Portraits of Wilderness

A Vision of Preservation

eco corps

1585-A Folsom Street, San Francisco, California 94103

Tel: 415-522-1680 FAX: 415-626 1510

email: portraits@ecocorps.org

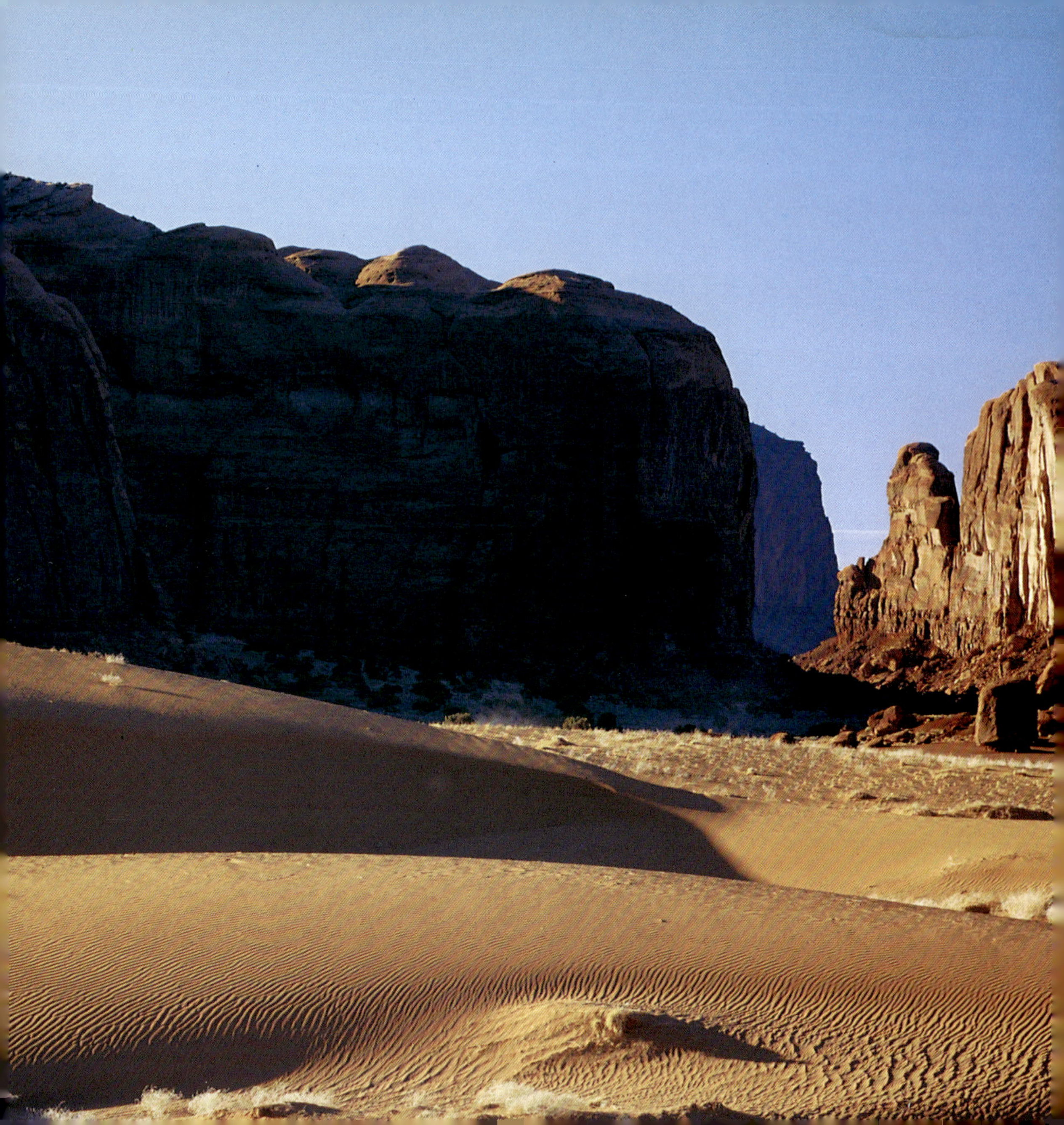

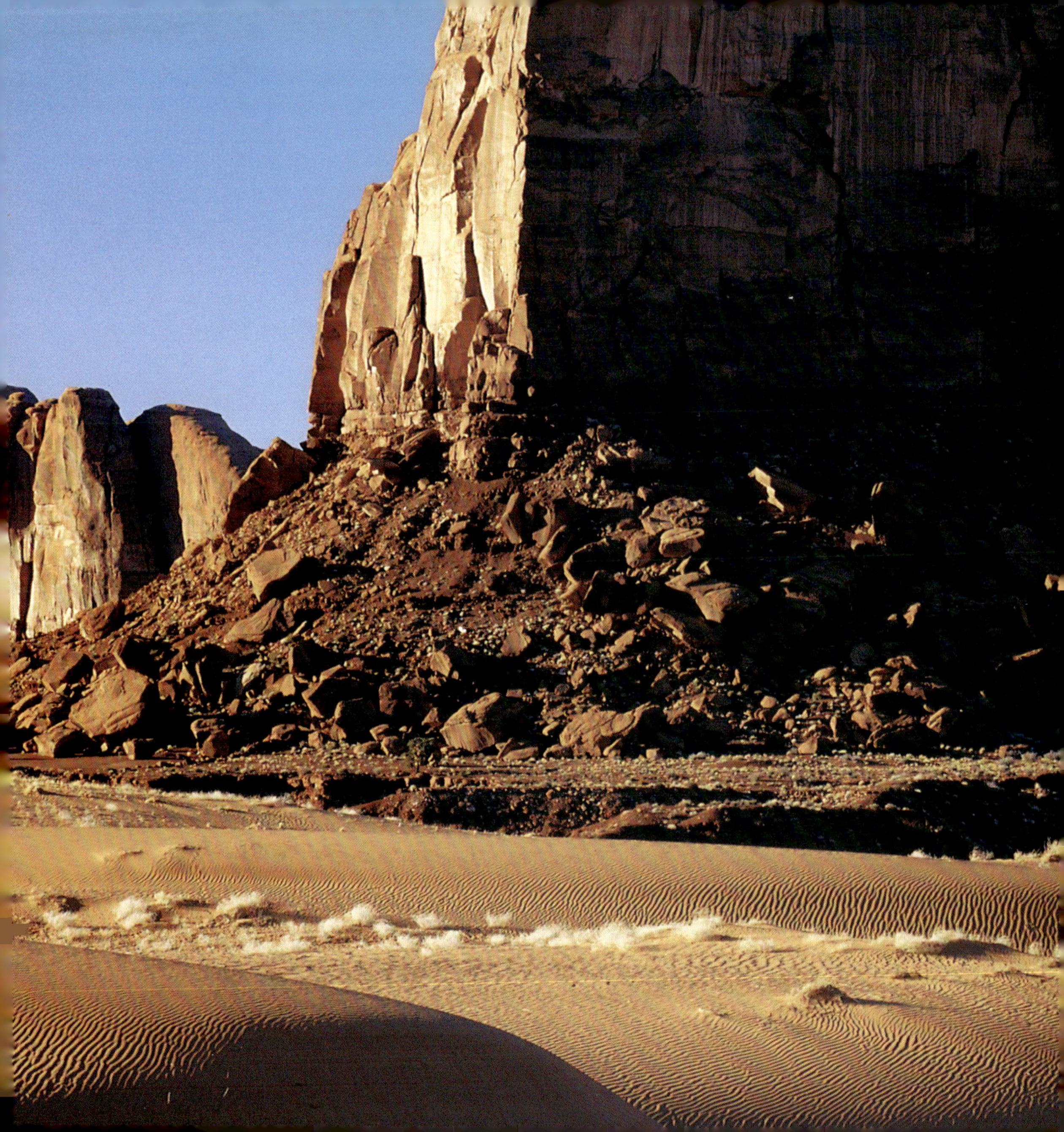

Photography by Bruce Heinemann

ISBN 0-945475-07-1

1585-A Folsom Street
San Francisco, California 94103
415.522.1680 Fax: 415.626.1510
E-Mail: *portraits@ecocorps.org*

Printed in Hong Kong By Palace Press International, San Francisco

♲ Printed on Recycled Paper
In recognition of our shared responsibility to preserve the environment
Palace Press International will plant double the trees
to replace every tree that was harvested
to produce the paper to make this book.

Introduction

na-ture (nā cher) n. 1. The order, disposition, and essence of all entities composing the physical universe. 2. The forces or processes of the physical world. 3. The primitive state of existence, untouched and uninfluenced by civilization or artificiality. 4. Reality, as distinguished from the imaginary.

The American Heritage Dictionary

When we speak of the environment we call it "nature." We seek to define and pigeonhole that which is undefinable and unknowable in all its aspects. We call our collective existence by such names as *society*, *culture*, *race*, or by *country*, *city*, or *town*. But these definitions are superficial. Nature is that giant force, that global being, which sustains our existence. We see it between the street and the sidewalk, confined to parks which are surrounded by asphalt, yards with mowed grass and potted flowers, or that strip of land next to the highway. We attempt to disengage ourselves from nature and thus make our artificial existence acceptable. In reality, this is like separating ourselves from our bodies. It only can be achieved in death.

Similarly, our separation from the planet is like death. Some say, wisely, that we are not our bodies. Yet we know from experience that abusing our bodies causes suffering. In the same way, abusing the earth causes suffering, not just for us but for all other living beings.

When we look at the images herein we should understand that these are the real measures of wealth in any society. To sacrifice our air, water, food, natural beauty, and open space in the name of pursuing a higher standard of living would be foolish. As Henry David Thoreau asks, "What is the use of a house without a tolerable world to build it on?" Yet America's natural heritage—our old-growth forests, our pristine lakes and streams, our rich and vast farmlands, our abundant and diverse wildlife—is being destroyed at an alarming rate even as we view the photographs in this book.

EcoCorps wants to make environmental awareness part of everyone's daily thinking. Before purchasing a product we should ask, "How will this effect the earth?" When we vote we should consider, "Will this person contribute to the preservation or destruction of the environment?" Before doing business, we should question, "What is this company's environmental track record?" And we should ask ourselves how our diet and lifestyle affect the natural world. Unless we all start asking these questions and answering them honestly, our natural resources will vanish.

Consumption has become the measure of success and the Earth is paying the price. EcoCorps believes that ecological consciousness must become an inseparable part of American culture. To promote environmental awareness, EcoCorps is involved in numerous projects. *Ocean Song Farm and Wilderness Center* serves as an organic farm, environmental education center, wilderness preserve and retreat facility. Located on 340 acres in the coastal hills of California's Sonoma County, *Ocean Song* is a practical example of sustainable living.

To restore and preserve one of Hawaii's most precious coastal areas, EcoCorps is developing the *Waipio Valley Arboretum*, a 42-acre arboretum and ecocultural garden retreat on the Hamakua Coast. Alternative agricultural techniques such as organic gardening, bamboo cultivation, and permaculture are employed and are the topics of seminars and field training. A museum of cultural history in Waipio Valley and a Hamakua orientation center will serve as a community support facility. The arboretum and garden will feature indigenous tropicals and endangered exotic species of plants. Cultural gardens and structures will showcase traditions of sound ecological stewardship.

In India, EcoCorps is restoring and preserving damaged ecosystems, ancient shrines, and historic architectural sites. By publishing books, creating video documentaries, and working with individuals and organizations, EcoCorps is informing people worldwide of the critical issues that are affecting the culture and environment of the people of India.

In order to direct people's purchases to environmentally responsible products and services we have formed the *Green Consumer Co-op* a clearinghouse of earth-friendly products. EcoCorps is also distributing literature and audio/visual materials at schools and other public places, as well as conducting workshops and seminars on topics ranging from straw-bale construction to vegetarian cooking. By organizing grass-roots campaigns EcoCorps is keeping people informed of environmental issues and offering practical solutions to the problems we face.

Join EcoCorps in its battle to inform and preserve.

Jill Tabler, *Director, EcoCorps*

EcoCorps
1585 A Folsom Street, San Francisco, CA 94103
Tele: (415) 522-1680 Fax: (415) 626-1510
email: portraits@ecocorps.org

COME FORTH into the light of things,
Let Nature be your Teacher...

One impulse from a vernal wood
May teach you more of man,
Of moral evil and of good,
Than all the sages can...

Enough of Science and of Art;
Close up those barren leaves;
Come forth, and bring with you a heart
That watches and receives.

William Wordsworth

Sunset in Canyonlands National Park, Utah

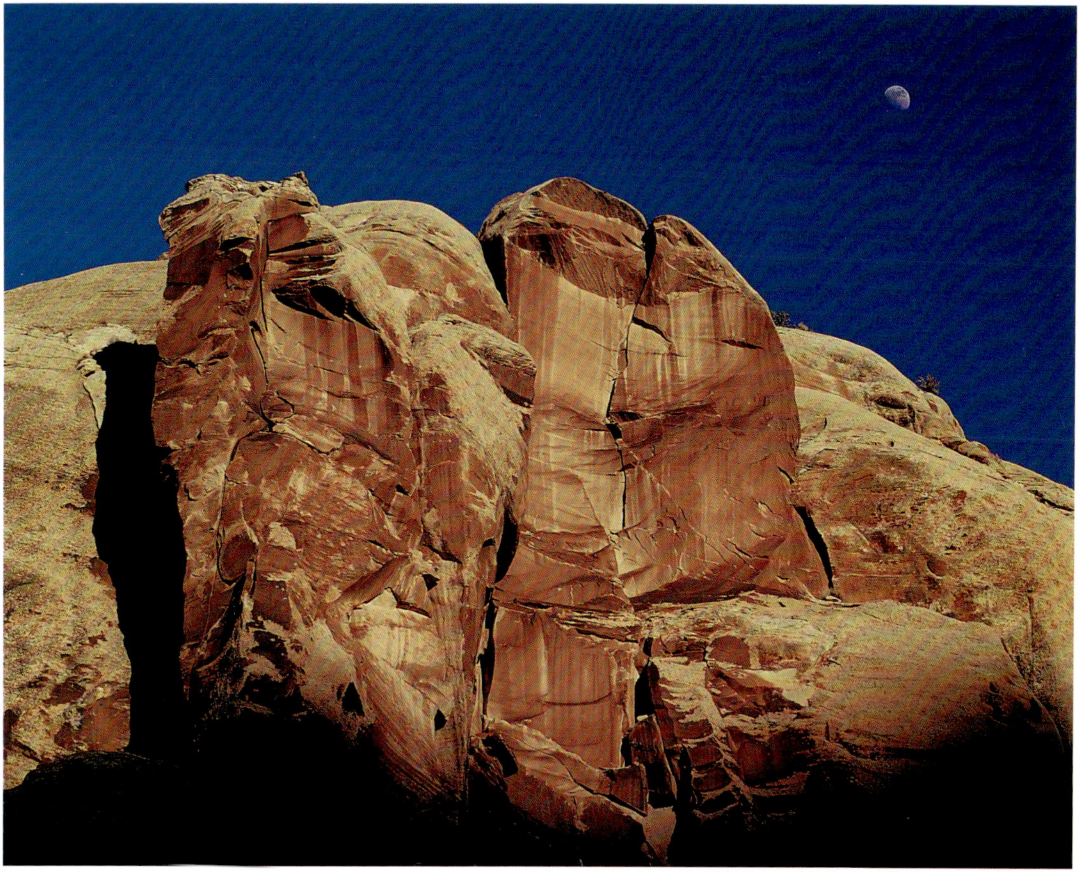

I WILL ARISE AND GO NOW, and go to Innisfree,
And a small cabin build there, of clay and wattles made;
Nine bean-rows will I have there, a hive for the honey-bee,
And live alone in the bee-loud glade.

And I shall have some peace there, for peace comes dropping slow,
Dropping from the veils of the morning to where the cricket sings;
There midnight's all a glimmer, and noon a purple glow,
And evening full of the linnet's wings.

I will arise and go now, for always night and day
I hear lake water lapping with low sounds by the shore;
While I stand on the roadway, or on the pavements grey,
I hear it in the deep heart's core.

The Lake Isle of Innisfree/William Butler Yeats

Cedar Creek, Opal Creek Watershed, Oregon

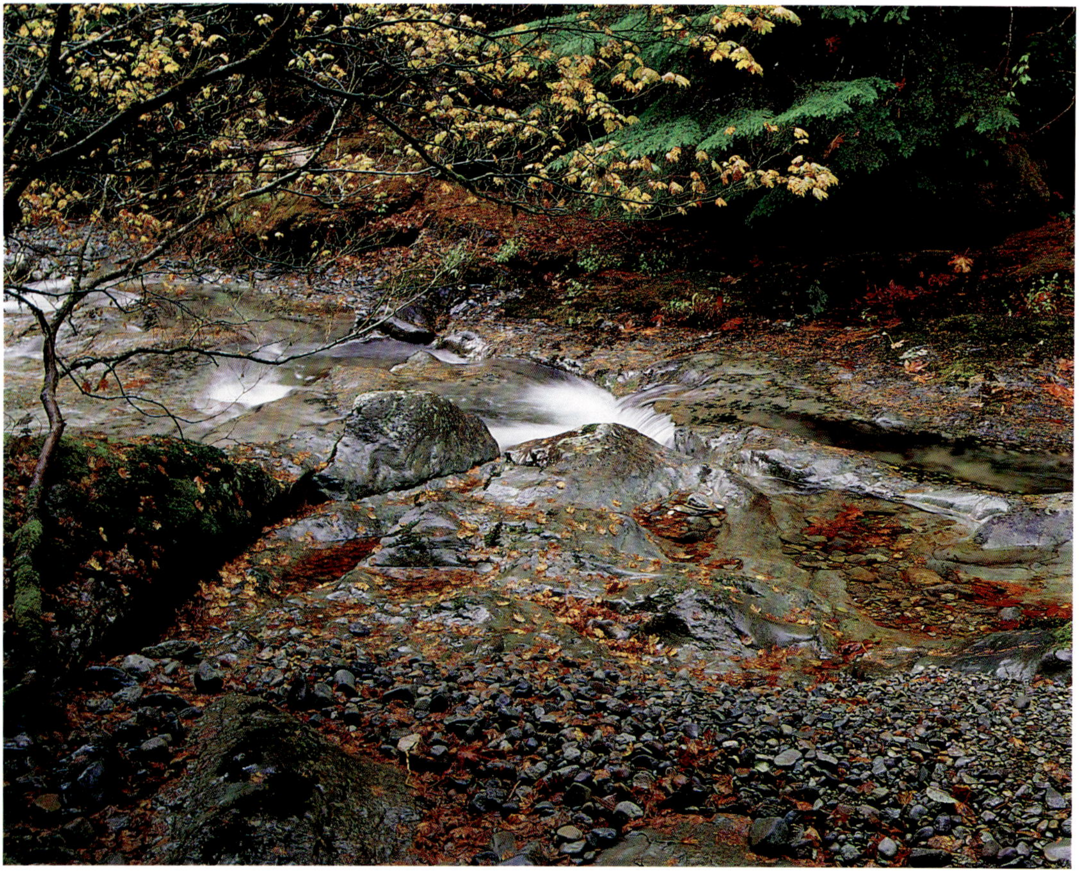

CONSIDER THE LIFE OF TREES.

Aside from the axe, what trees acquire from man is inconsiderable.

What man may acquire from trees is immeasurable.

From their mute forms there flows a poise, in silence;

a lovely sound and motion in response to wind.

What peace comes to those aware of the voice and bearing of trees!

Cedric Wright

Mount Ranier National Park

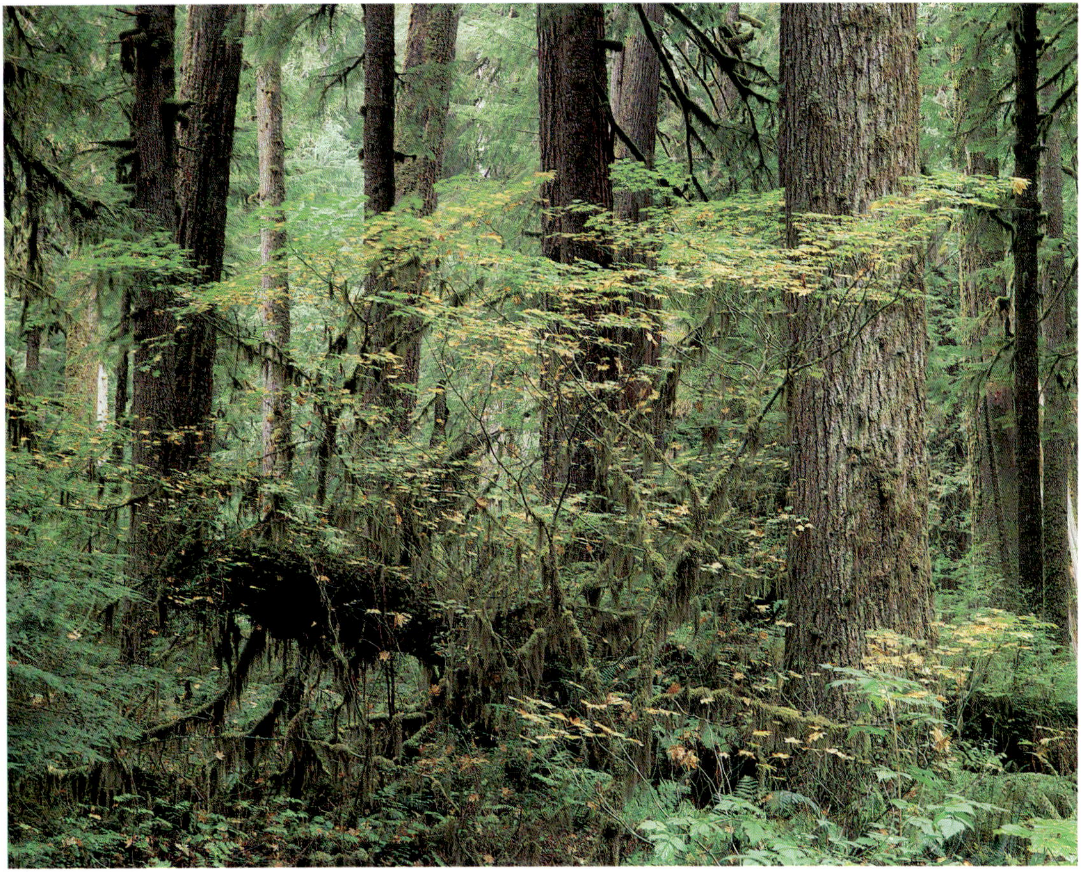

NATURE'S FIRST GREEN is gold,
Her hardest hue to hold.
Her early leaf's a flower;
But only so an hour.
Then leaf subsides to leaf.
So Eden sank to grief,
So dawn goes down to day.
Nothing gold can stay.

Robert Frost

North Cascades, Washington State

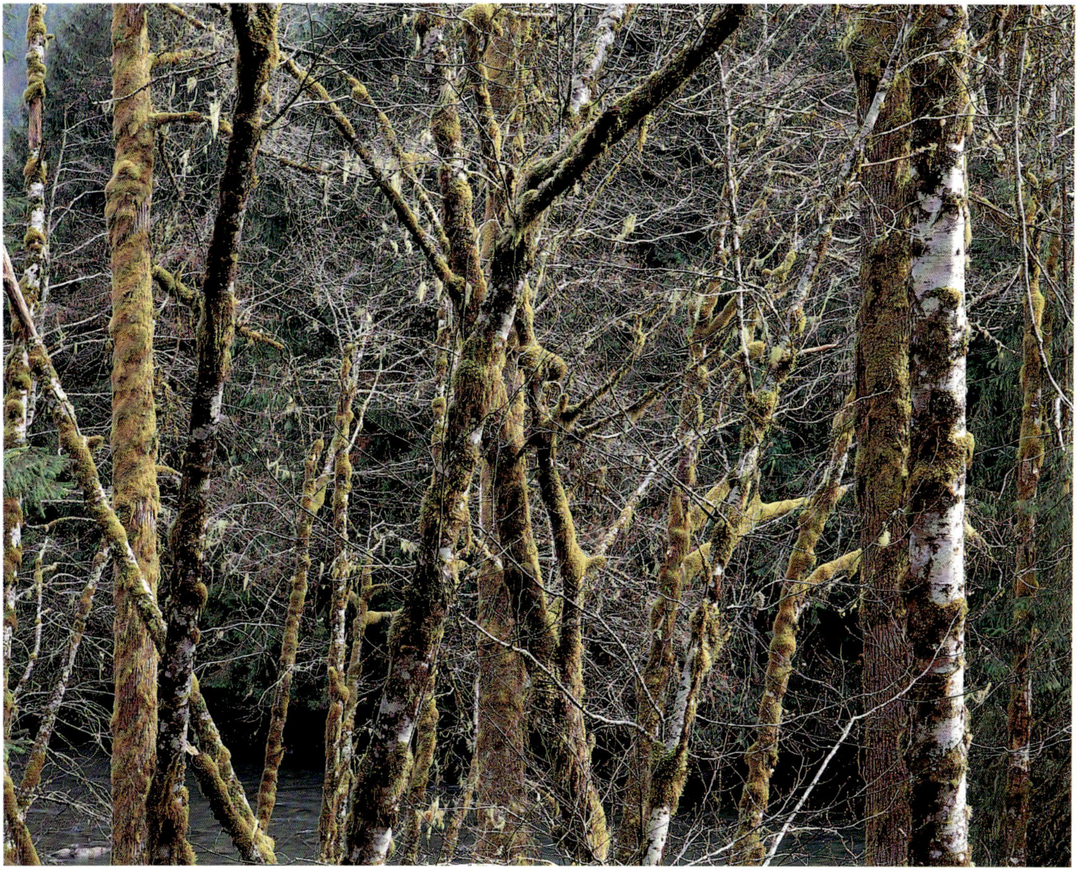

I AM THE TASTE of water,
the light of the sun and moon.
the sacred OM in all the Vedas,
the sound in ether,
and the ability in man.

Lord Krishna in the Bhagavad-Gita

Spring waterfall, Mt. Ranier National Park

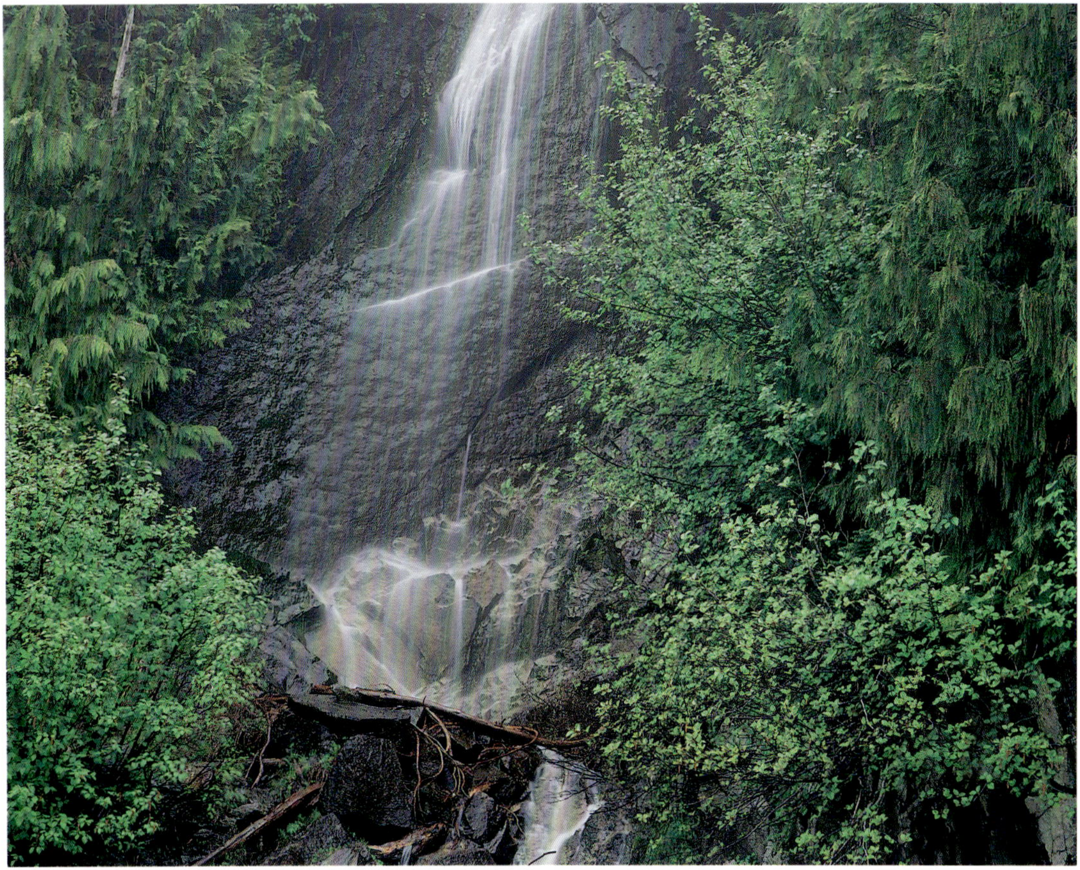

THE VISIBLE MARKS of extraordinary wisdom
and power appear so plainly in all the works of creation
that a rational creature who will but seriously reflect on them
cannot miss the discovery of a deity.

John Locke

Canyonlands National Park, Utah

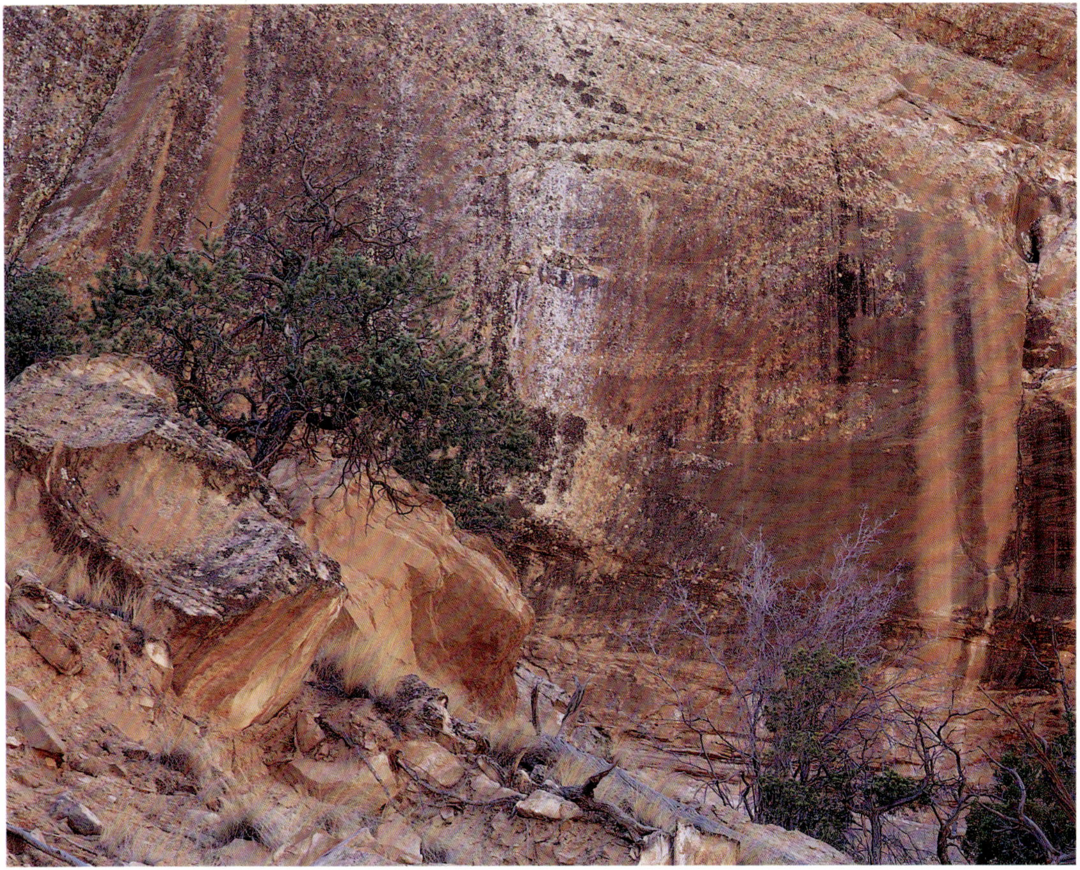

THERE IS RELIGION in everything around us,
A calm and holy religion
In the unbreathing things in Nature…
It is the poetry of Nature;
It is that which uplifts the spirit within us…
And which opens to our imagination
a world of spiritual beauty and holiness.

John Rushkin

Skate Creek, Washington State

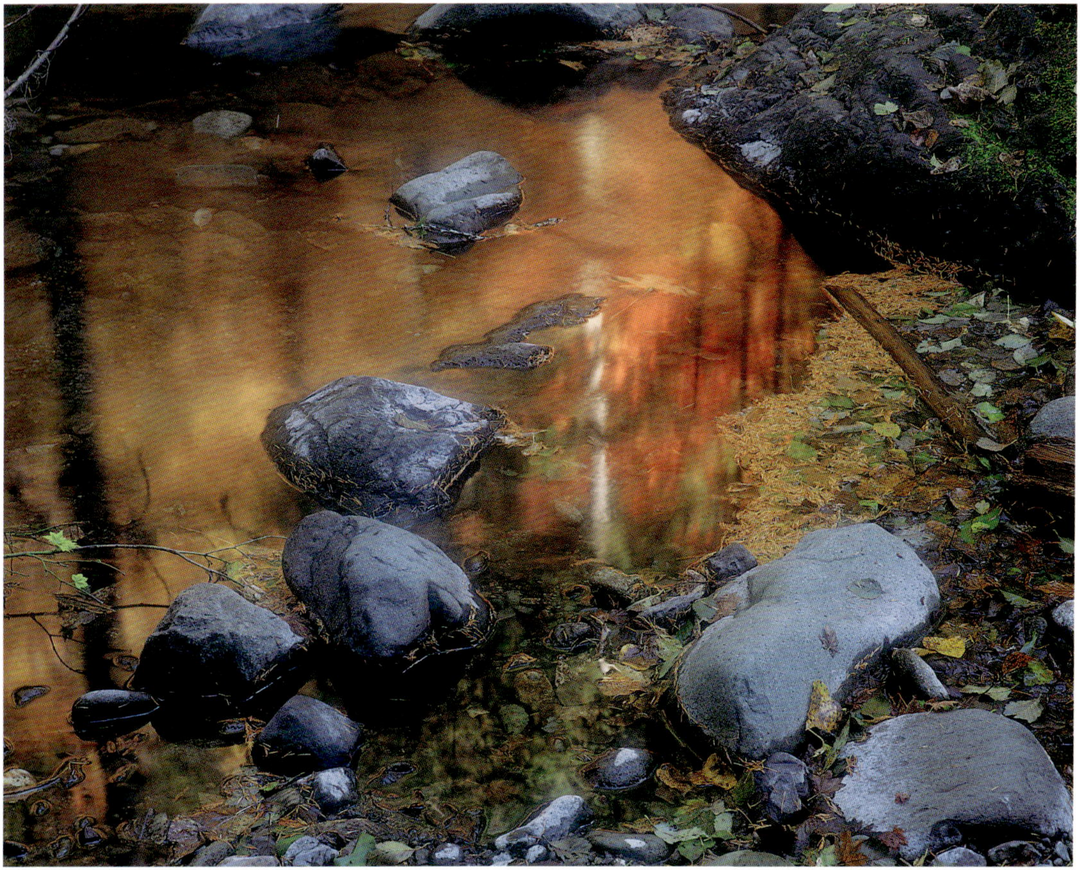

TO WASTE, to destroy our natural resources,
to skin and exhaust the land
instead of using it so as to increase its usefulness,
will result in undermining in the days of our children,
the very prosperity which we ought by right
to hand down to them amplified and developed.

Theodore Roosevelt

Ohanapecosh River, Mt. Ranier National Park, Washington State

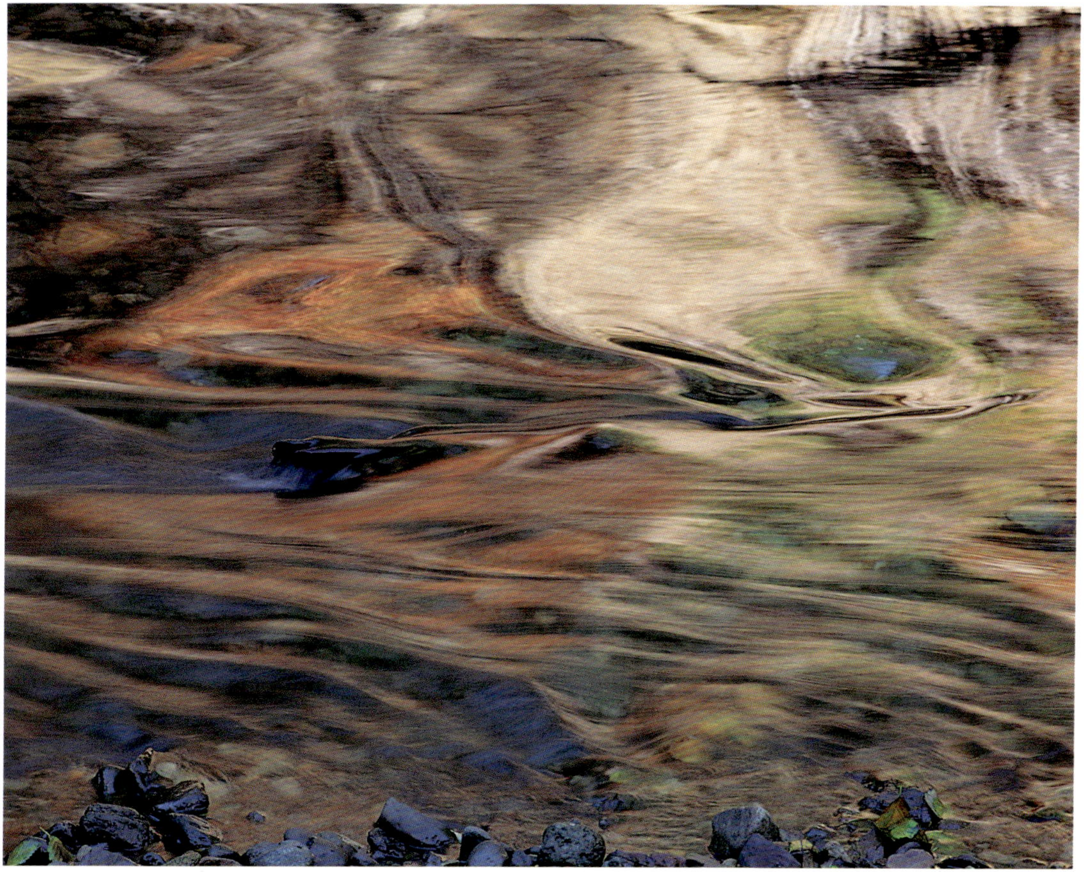

MY HELP is in the mountain
Where I take myself to heal
The earthly wounds
That people give to me.
I find a rock with sun on it
And a stream where the water runs gentle
And the trees which one by one give me company.

Nancy Wood

North Cascades, Washington State

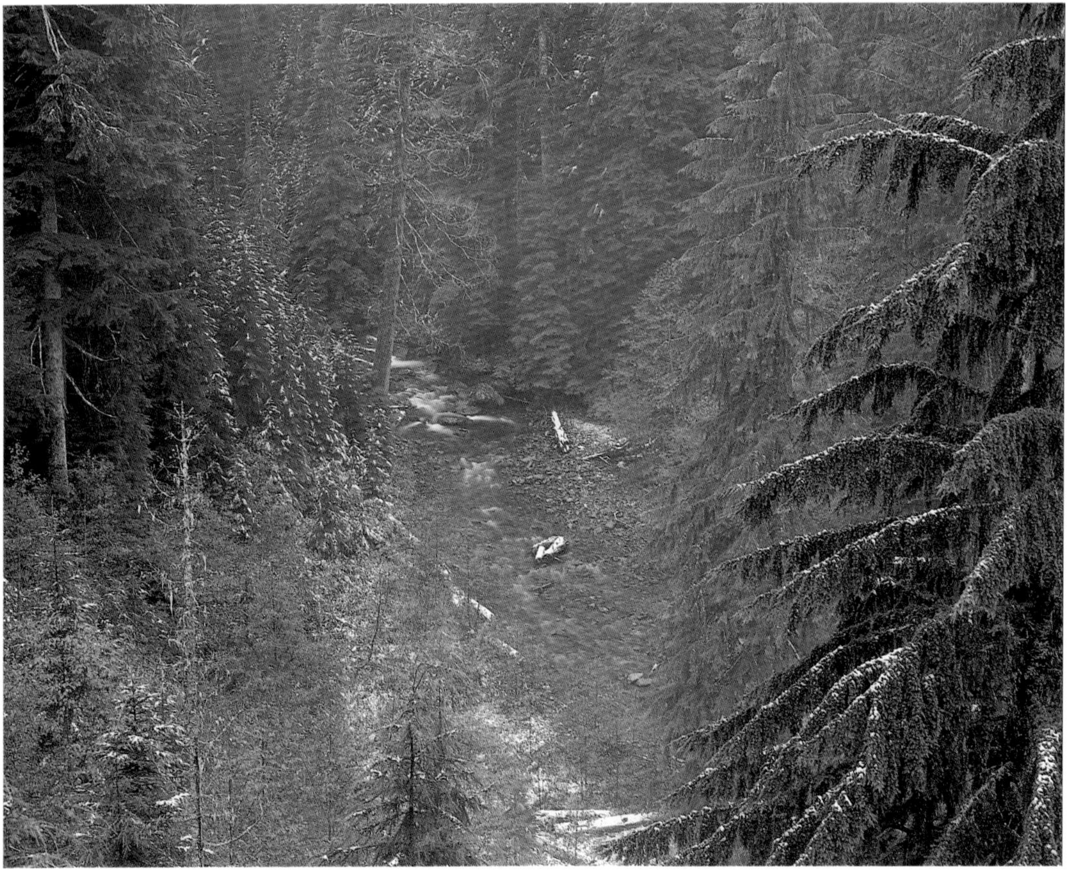

I SWEAR there is no greatness or power
that does not emulate those of the earth,
There can be no theory of any account
unless it corroborate the theory of the earth,
No politics, song, religion, behavior,
or what not, is of account, unless it compare
with the amplitude of the earth,
Unless it face the exactness, vitality,
impartiality, rectitude of the earth.

Walt Whitman

Oswald West State Park, Oregon Coast / Overleaf: Arches National Park, Utah

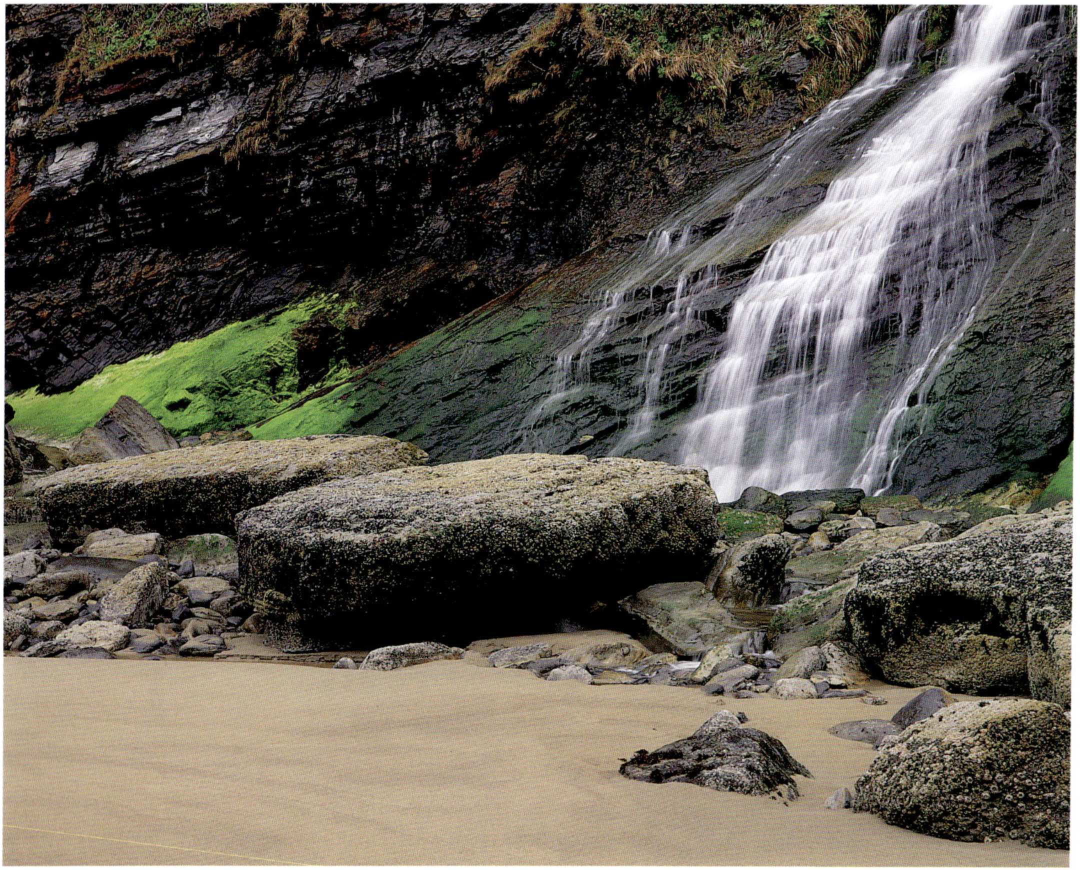

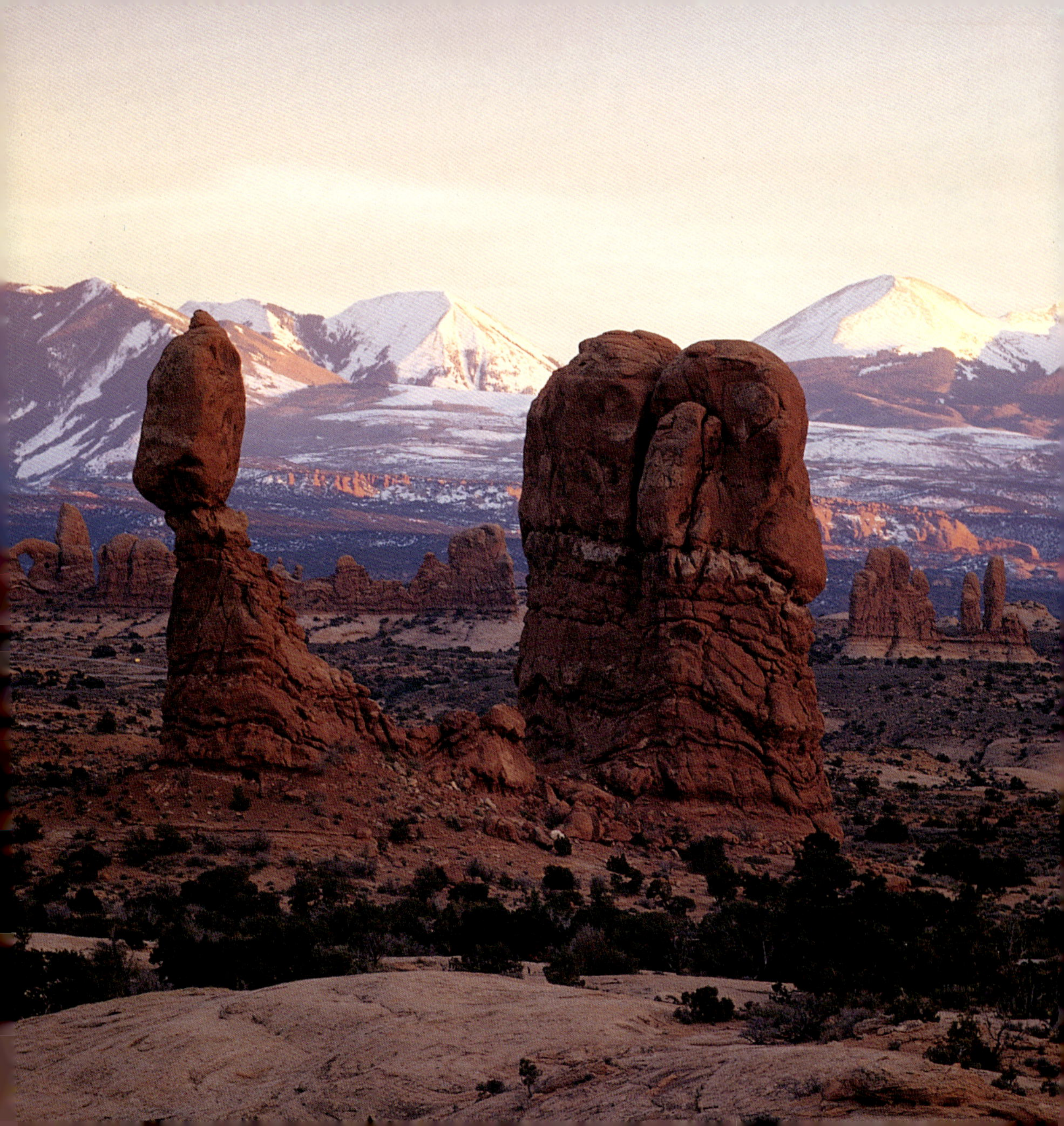

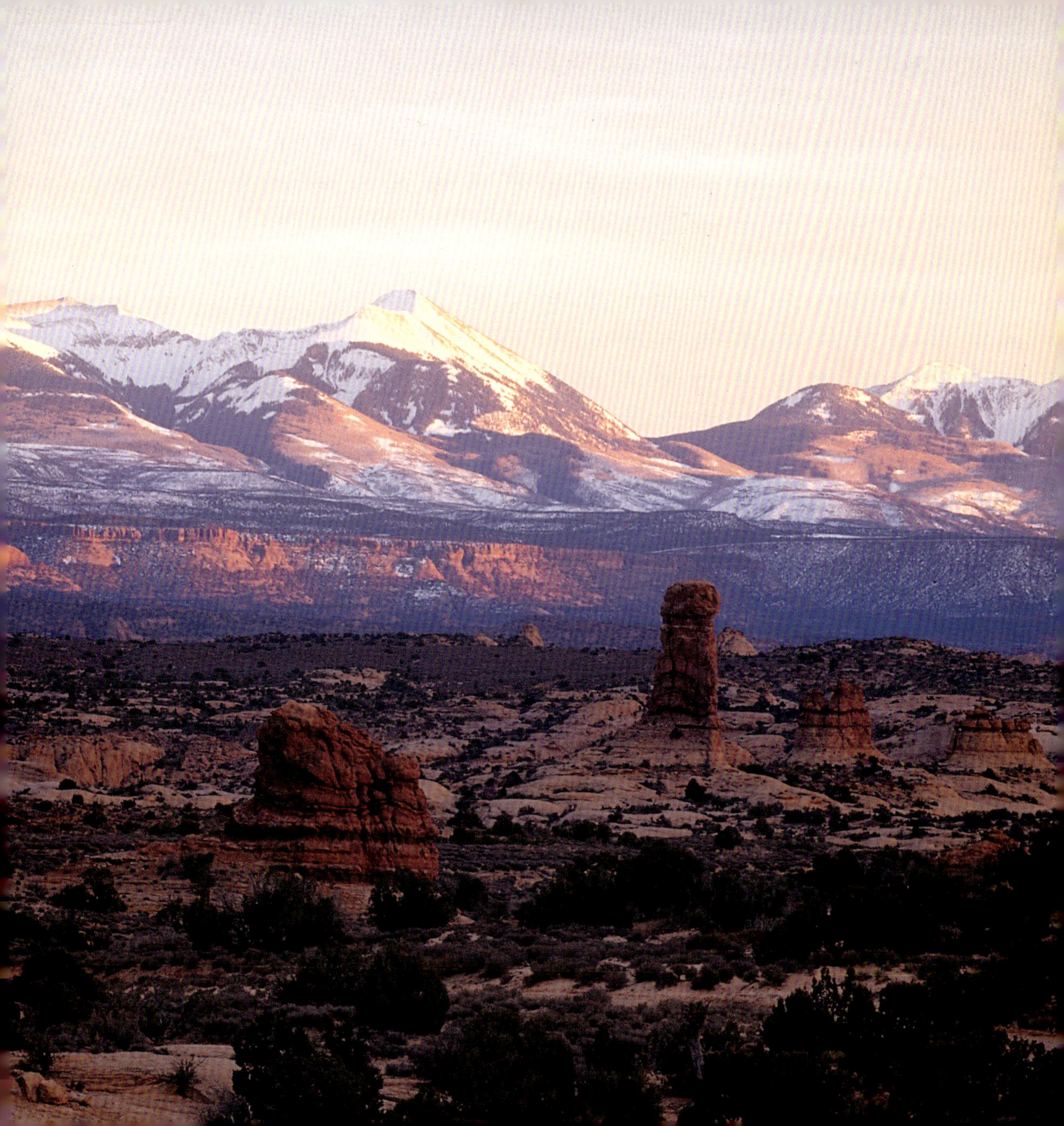

THE ENVIRONMENT IS FRIENDLY.

All adversities are favorable waves

pushing us and encouraging us

to move toward Divinity;

Reality the Beautiful.

Swami B. R. Sridhar

Falcon Cove, Oregon Coast

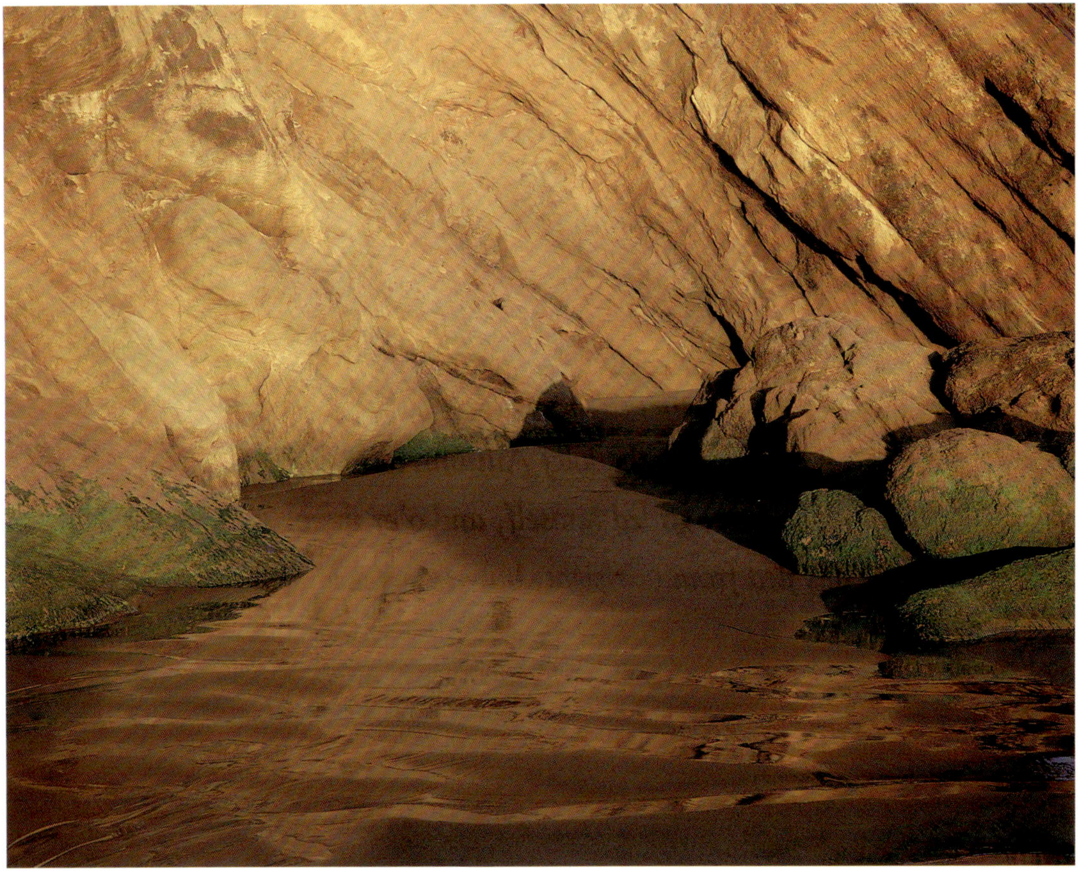

THE SPIRITS OF THE AIR *live on the smells*
Of fruit; and joy, with pinions light, roves round
The gardens, or sits singing in the trees."
Thus sang the jolly Autumn as he sat;
The rose, girded himself, and o'er the bleak
Hills fled from our sight; but left his golden load.

William Blake

Stillaquamish River, Washington State

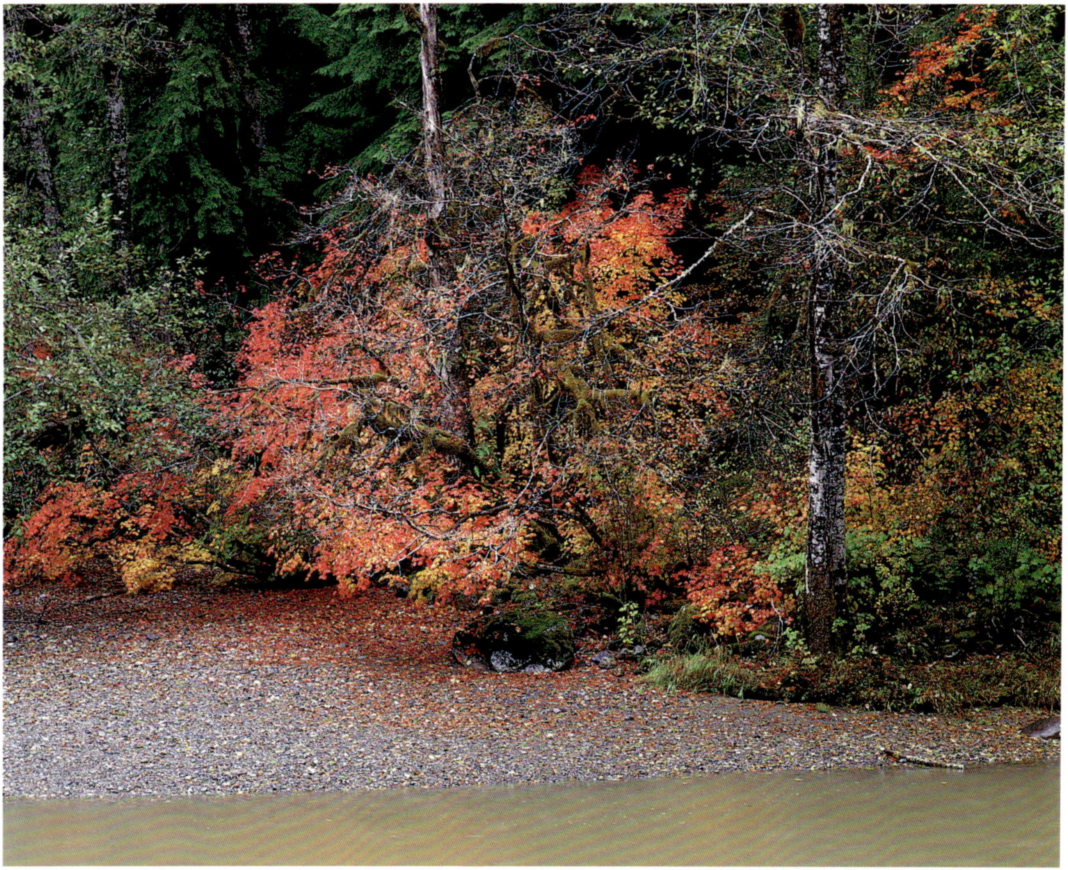

YOU ASK

why I perch
on a jade green mountain?
I laugh
but say nothing
my heart
free
like a peach blossom
in the flowing stream
going by
in the depths
in another world
not among men

Li Po

Opal Creek Preserve, Oregon

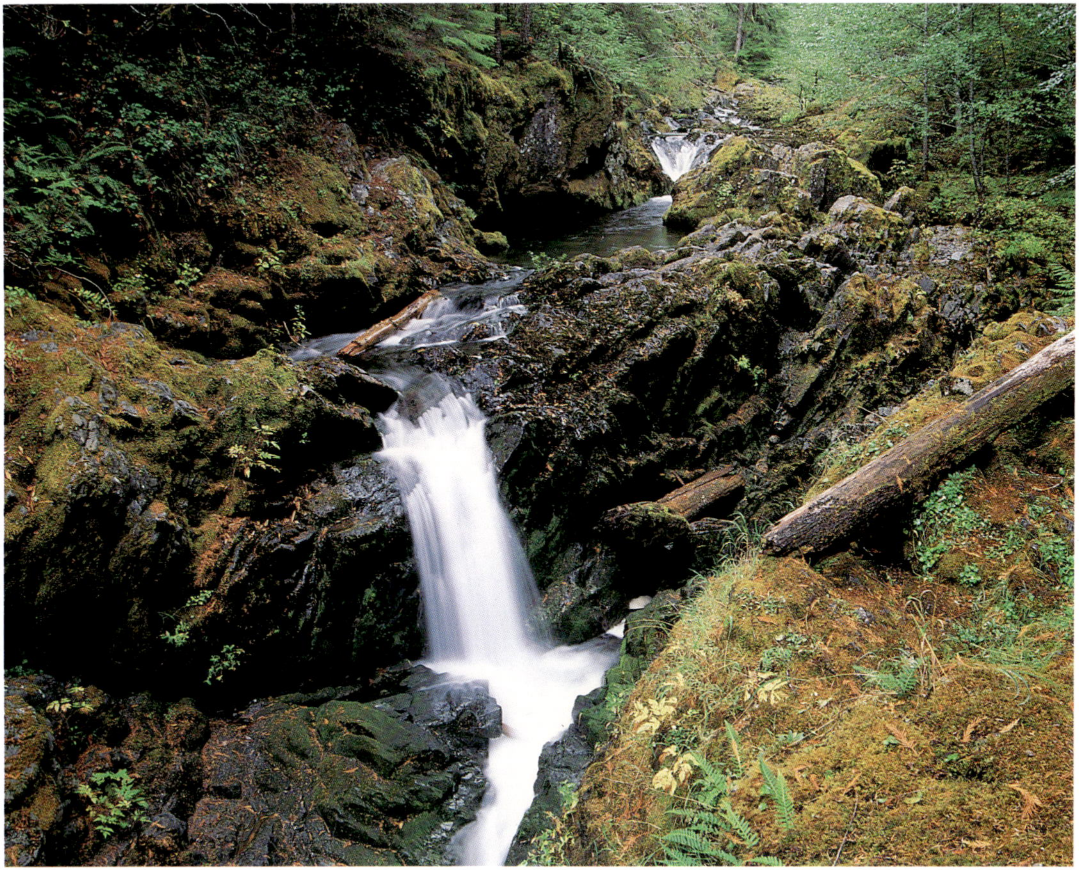

I HEARD a thousand blended notes,
While in a grove I sate reclined,
In that sweet mood when pleasant thoughts
Bring sad thoughts to the mind.

To her fair works did Nature link
The human soul that through me ran;
And much it grieved my heart to think
What man has made of man.

William Wordsworth

Opal Creek Preserve, Oregon

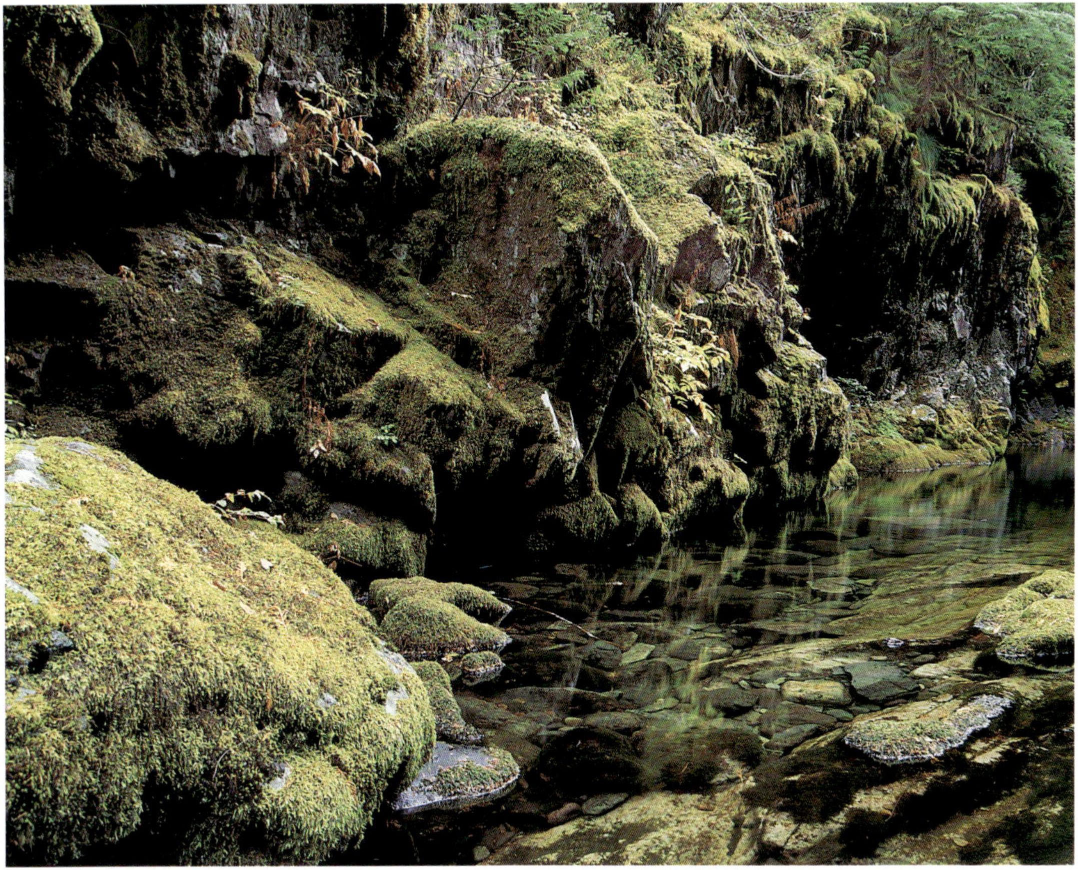

THE FORCE *that through the green fuse drives the flower*
Drives my green age; that blasts the roots of trees
Is my destroyer.
And I am dumb to tell the crooked rose
My youth is bent by the same wintry fever.

Dylan Thomas

North Cascades, Washington State / Overleaf: Monument Valley Arizona

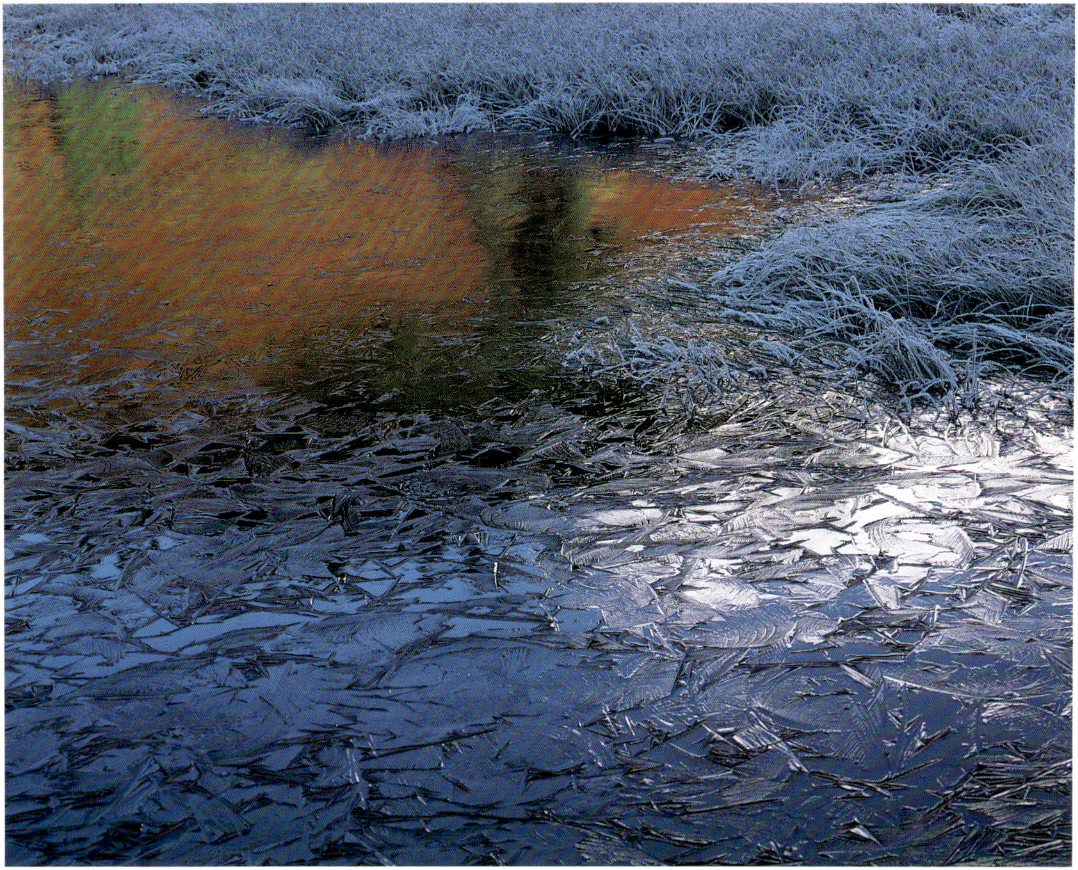

AH TO BE ALIVE

on a mid-September morn

fording a stream

barefoot, pants rolled up

sunshine, ice in the shallows,

northern rockies.

Rustle and shimmer of icy creek waters...

I pledge allegiance to the soil...

one ecosystem

in diversity

under the sun—

With joyful interpenetration for all.

Gary Snyder

Sauk River, Washington State

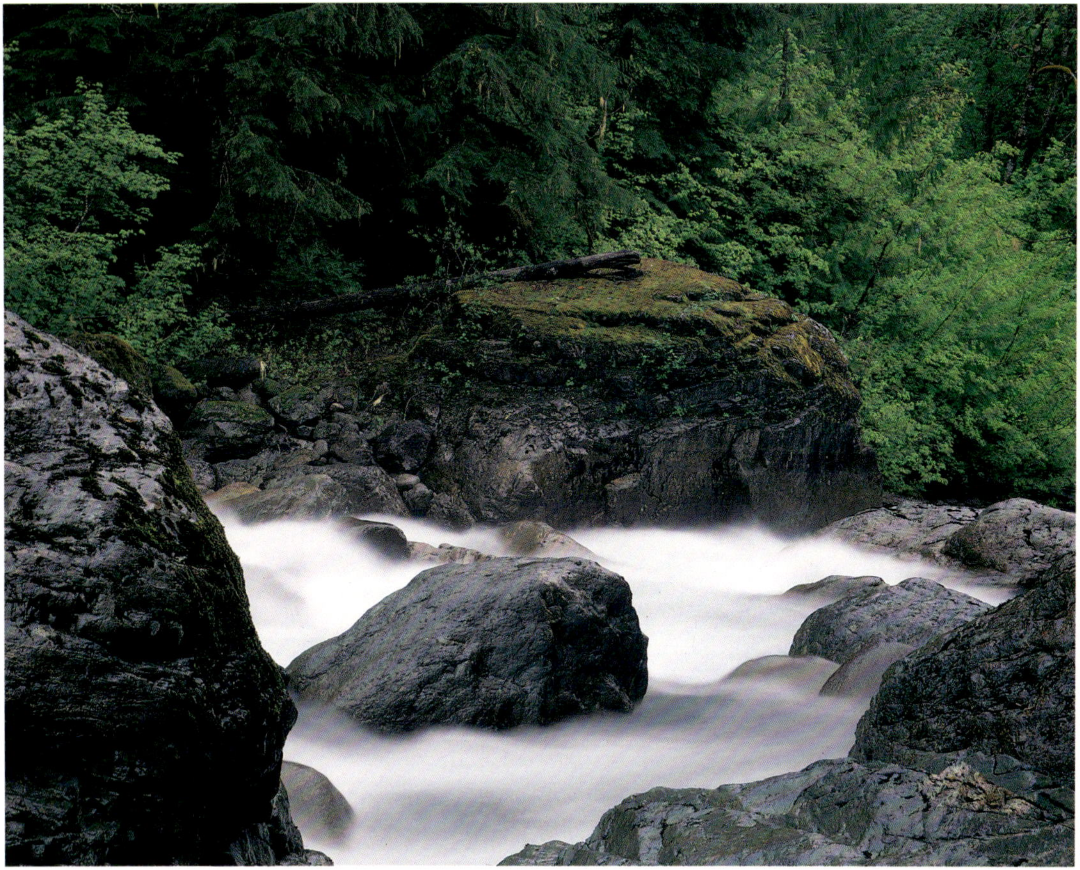

EVERY PART OF THIS SOIL IS SACRED
in the estimation of my people. Every hillside, every valley,
every plain and grove, has been hallowed by some sad or happy event
in the days long vanished. The very dust upon which you now stand responds
more lovingly to their footsteps than to yours,
because it is rich with the blood of our ancestors
and our bare feet are conscious of the sympathetic touch.

Chief Seattle

Blue Mountain, Utah / Overleaf: Monument Valley, Utah

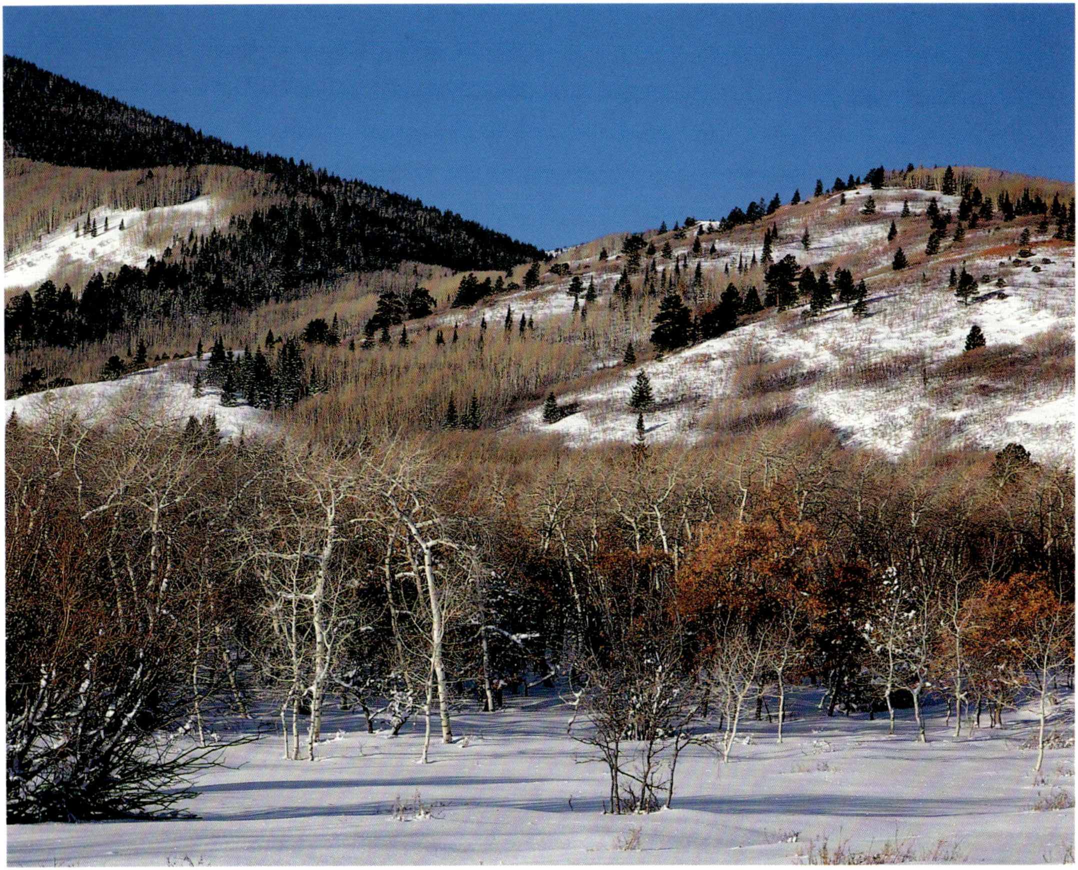

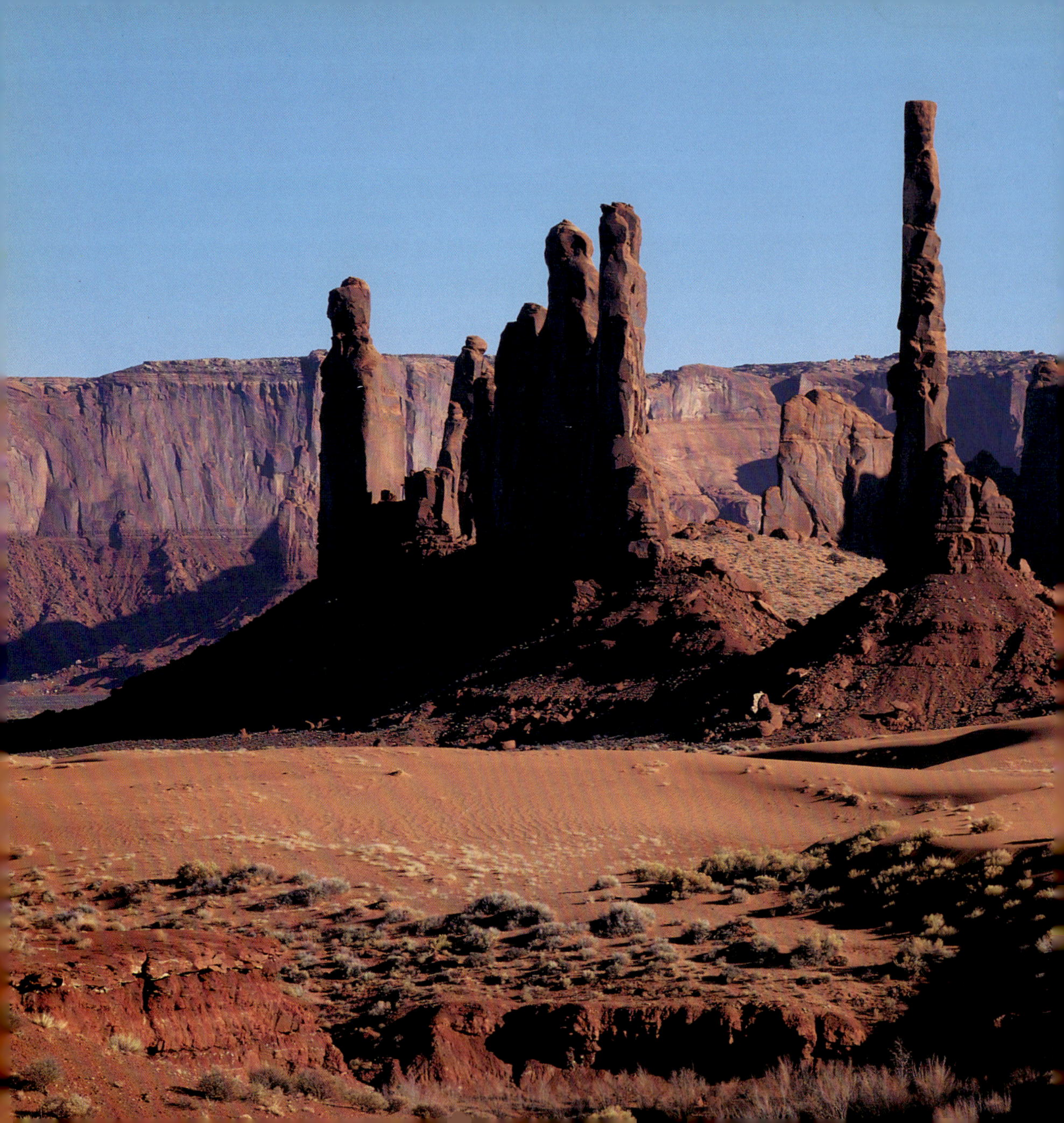

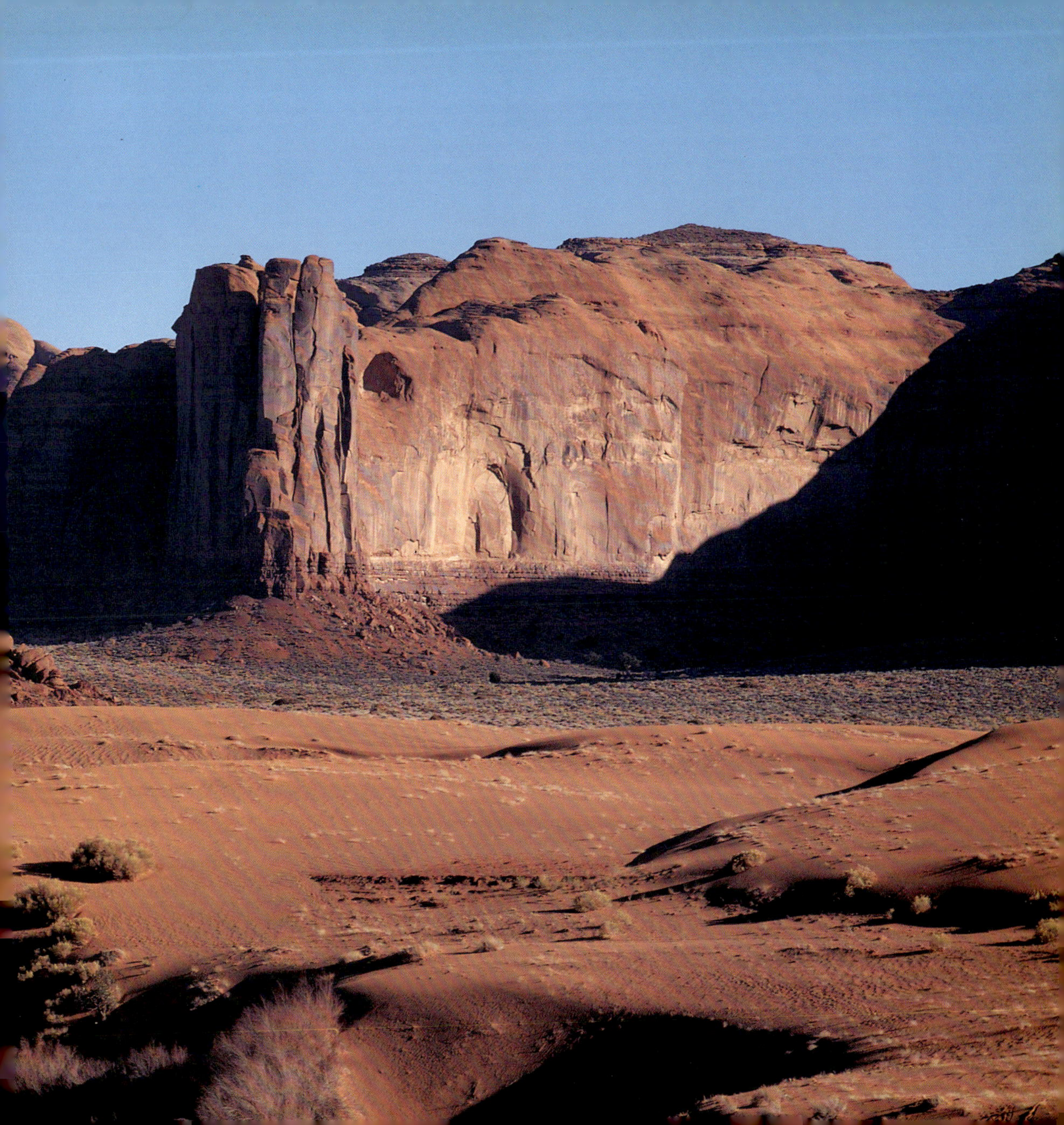

WE KNOW OURSELVES to be made from this earth.
We know this earth is made from our bodies.
For we see ourselves. And we are nature.
We are nature seeing nature.
We are nature with a concept of nature.
Nature weeping. Nature speaking of nature to nature.

Susan Griffin

North Cascades, Washington State

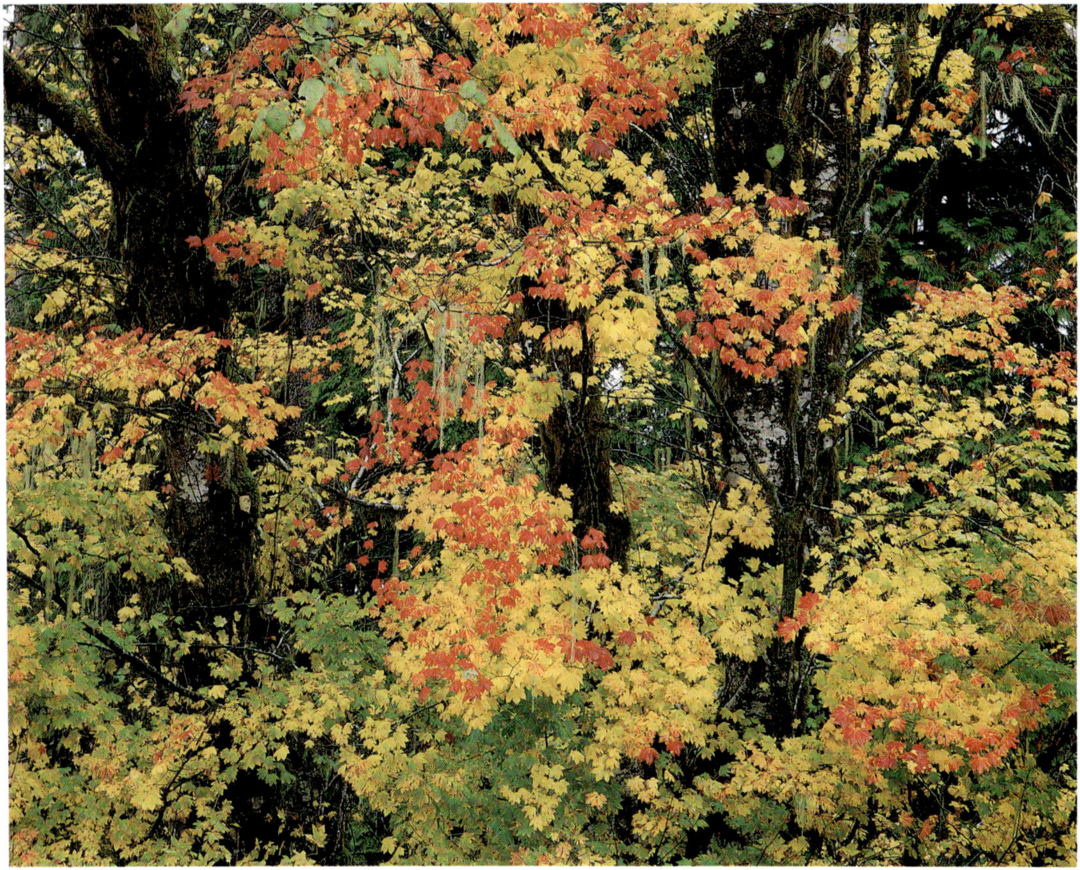

NATURE IS MIGHTY. *Art is mighty. Artifice is weak.*

For nature is the work of a mightier power than man.

Art is the work of man under the guidance

and inspiration of a mightier power.

Artifice is the work of mere man

in the imbecility of his mimic understanding.

Anon

Lake Powell, Utah

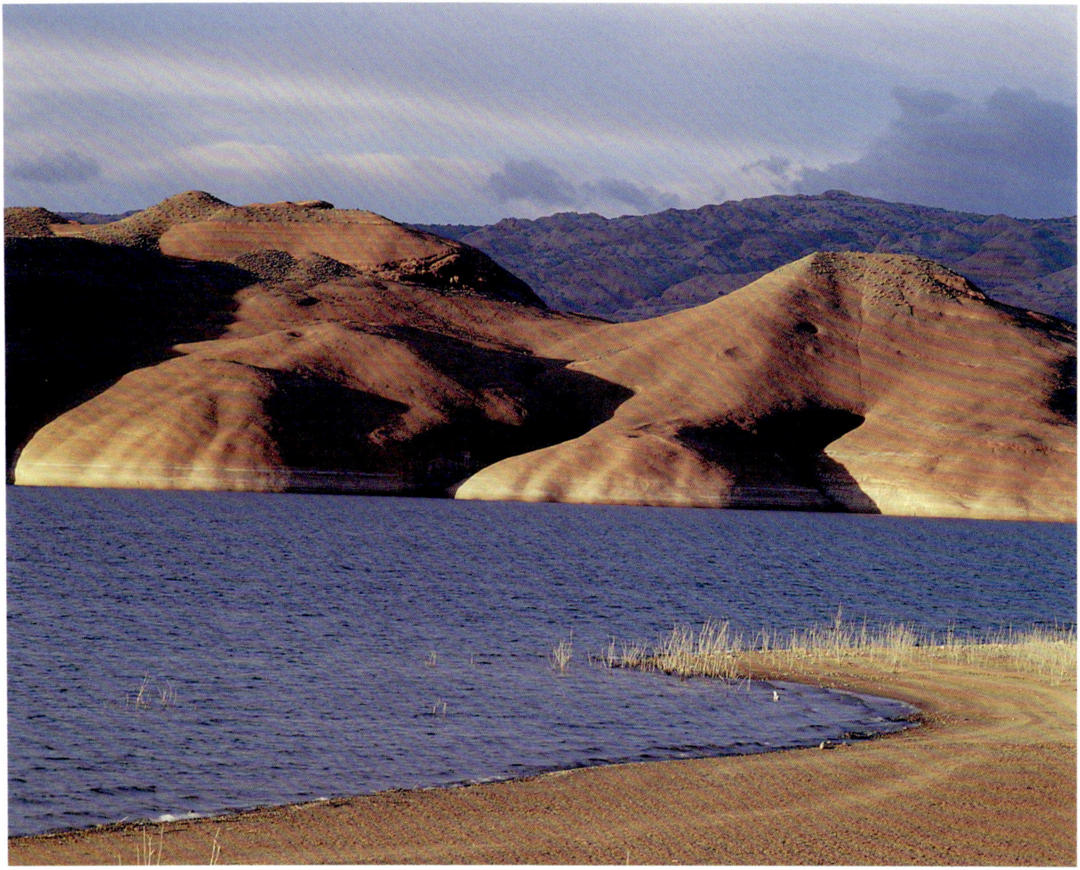

I PART THE OUT thrusting branches
and come in beneath
the blessed and the blessing trees.
Though I am silent
there is singing around me.
Though I am dark
there is vision around me.
Though I am heavy
there is flight around me.

Wendell Berry

Mt. Ranier National Park, Washington State

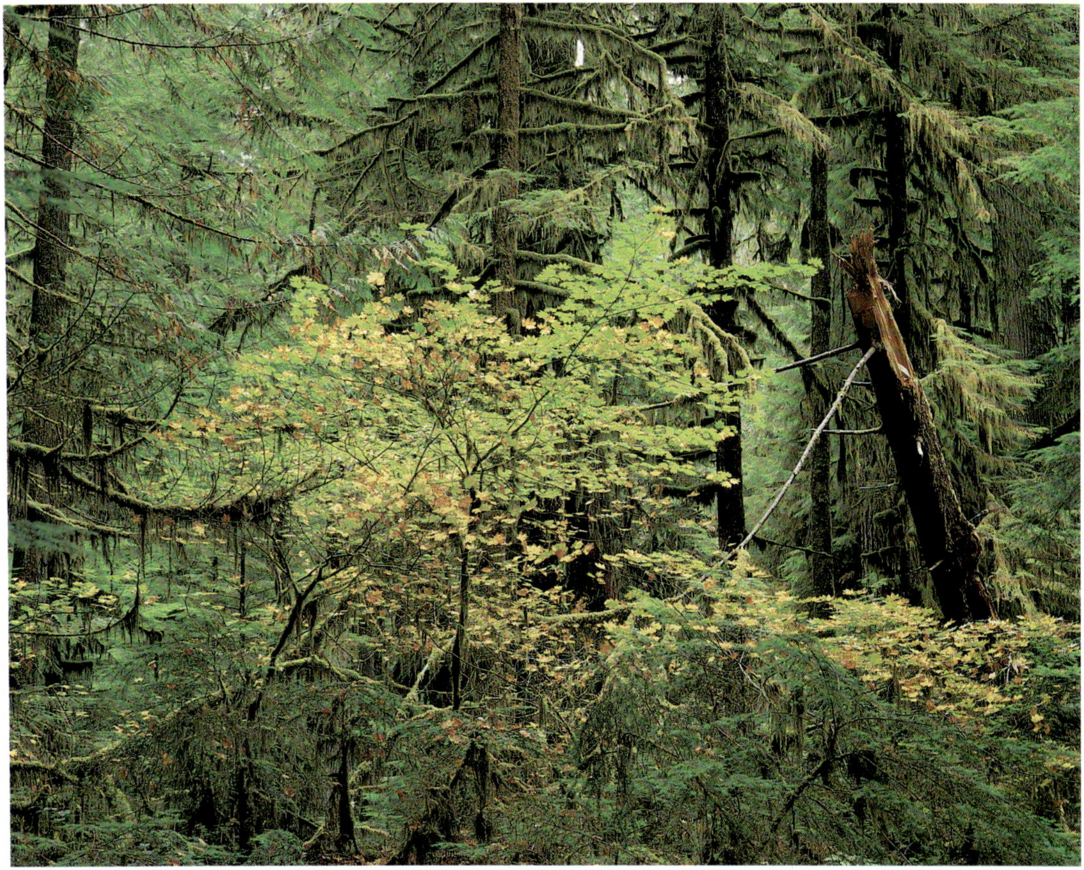

LET CHILDREN WALK with nature,
let them see the beautiful blendings
and communions of death and life,
their joyous inseparable unity,
as taught in woods and meadows,
plains and mountains,
and streams of our blessed star,
and they will learn that death is stingless indeed,
and as beautiful as life,
and that the grave has no victory,
for it never fights.
All is divine harmony.

John Muir

North Cascades, Washington State

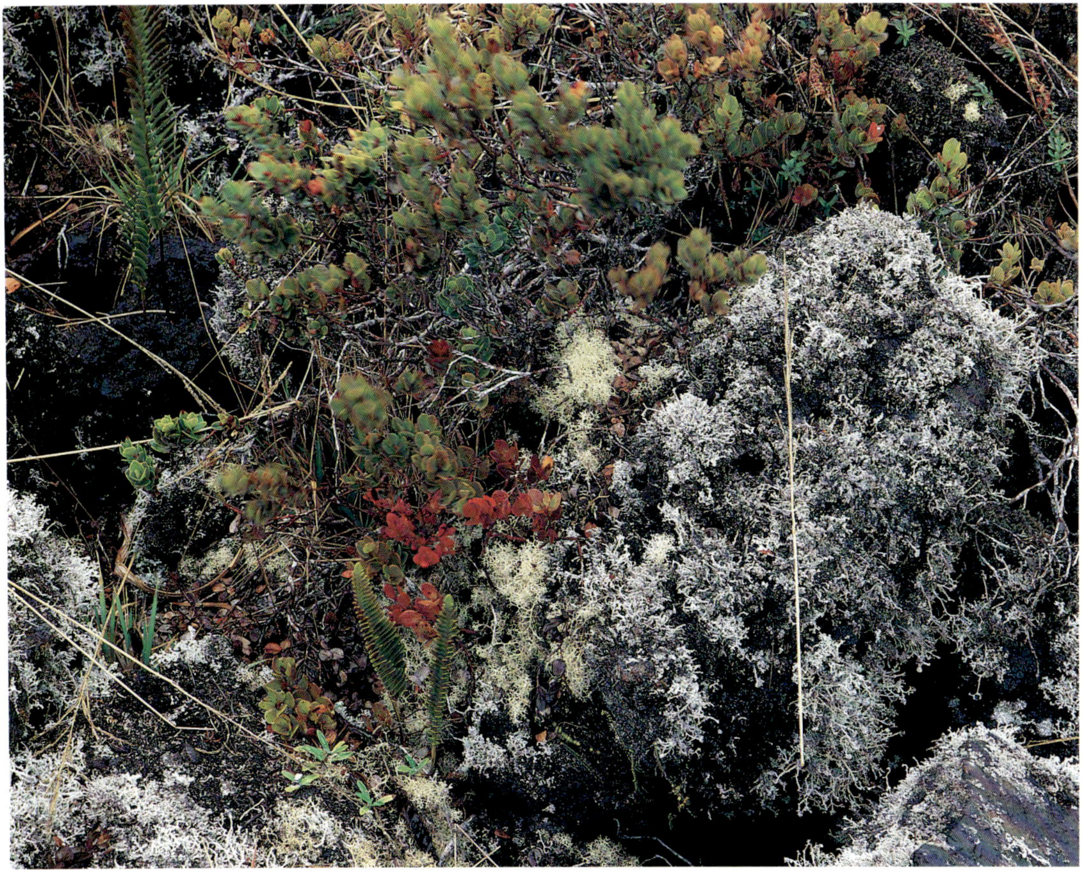

In the great Assembly of the Lotus all are present
Without divisions.
Grass, trees, the soil on which these grow
all have the same kinds of atoms.
Some are barely in motion
While others make haste along the path,
but they will all in time
Reach the Precious Island of Nirvana
Who can really maintain
That things inanimate lack buddhahood?

Chan-Jan

Rialto Beach, Washington Coast

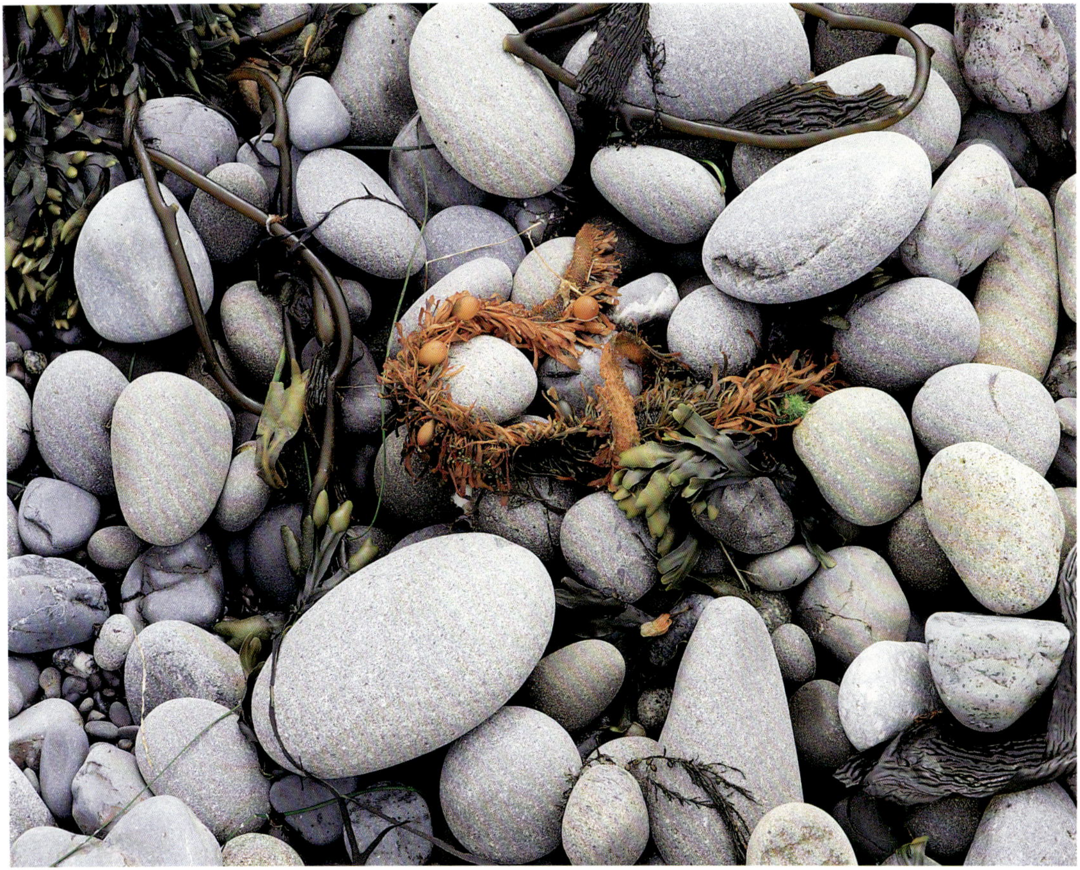

NATURE REACHES OUT TO US
with welcoming arms and bids us enjoy her beauty;
but we dread her silence and rush into the crowded cities,
there to huddle like sheep, fleeing from a ferocious wolf.

Kahlil Gibran

Opal Creek Preserve, Oregon

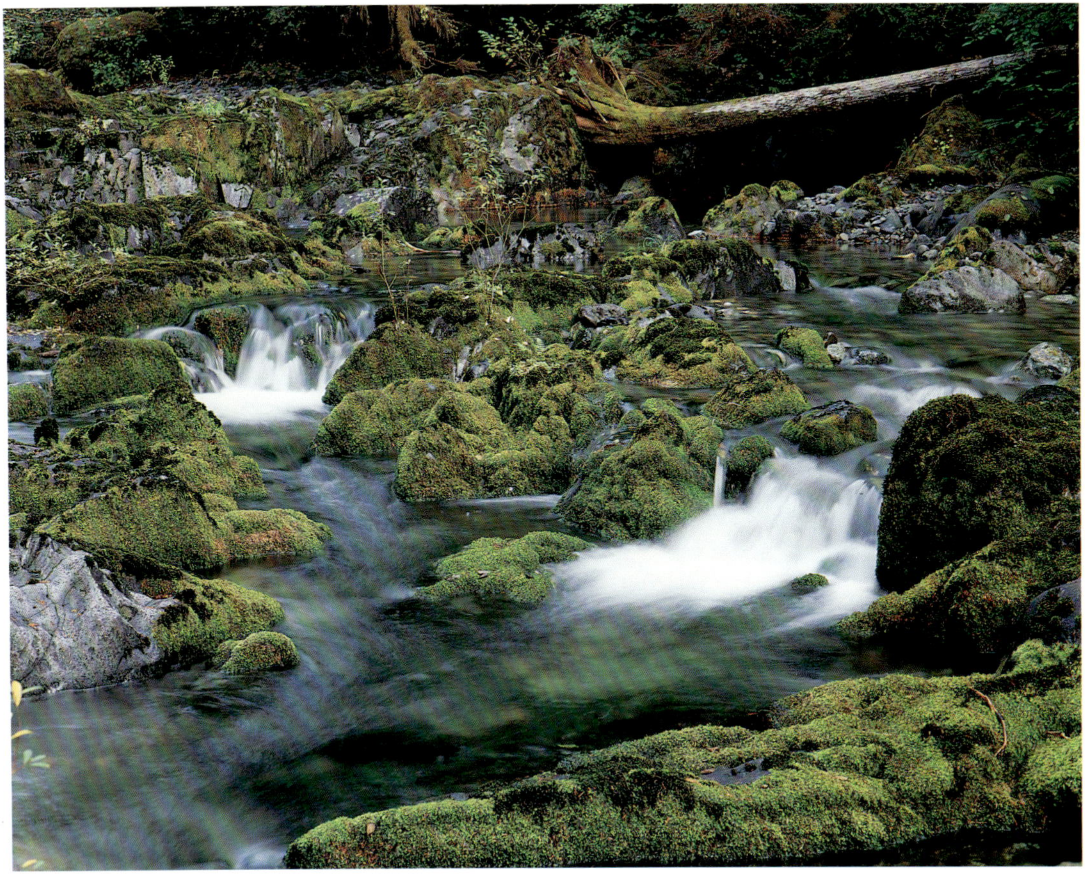

BLESSED sister, holy mother, spirit of the fountain,
spirit of the garden,
Suffer us not to mock ourselves with falsehood
Teach us to care and not to care
Teach us to sit still
Even among the rocks.
Our peace in his will
And even among these rocks
Sister, mother,
And spirit of the river, spirit of the sea.
Suffer me not to be separated
And let my cry come unto Thee.

T.S. Eliot

Oswald West State Park, Oregon Coast

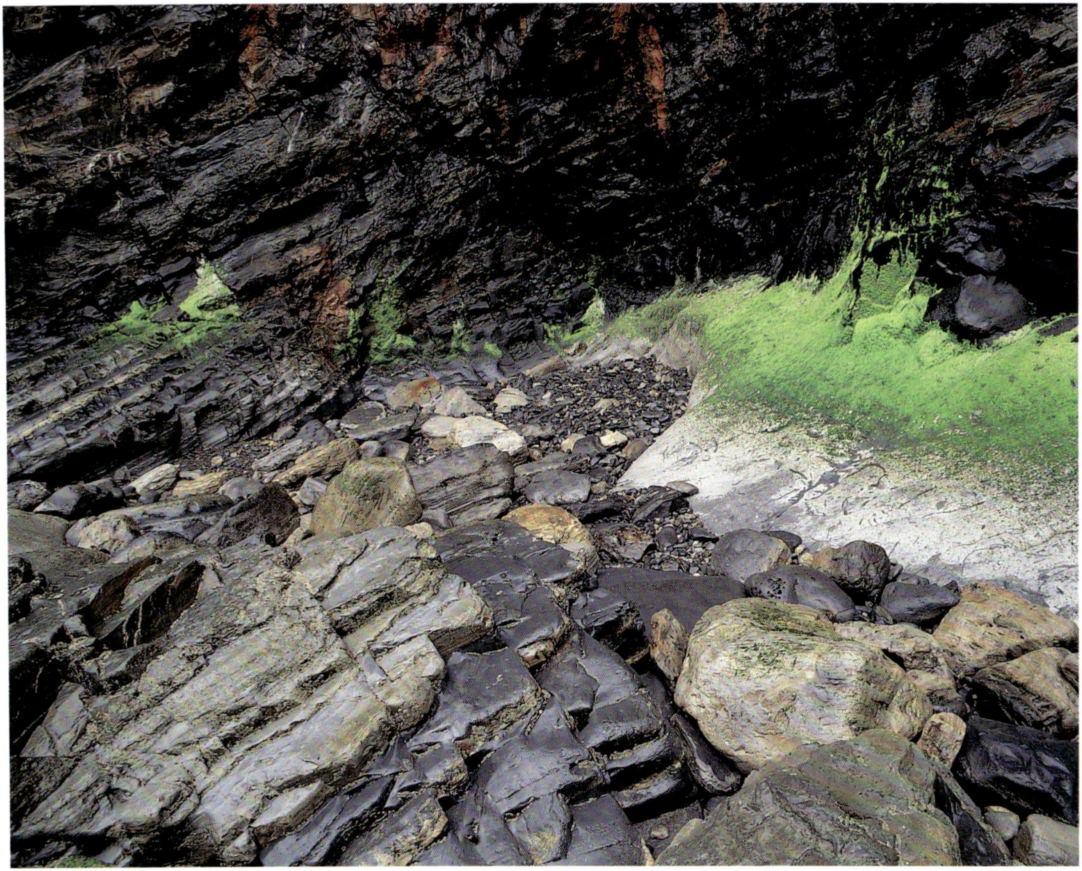

THE BOAST OF HERALDRY, *the pomp of power,*
And all that beauty, all that wealth e'er gave,
Awaits alike the inevitable hour.
The paths of glory lead but to the grave.
Thomas Gray

Bryce Canyon National Park, Utah / Overleaf: Falcon Cove, Oregon Coast

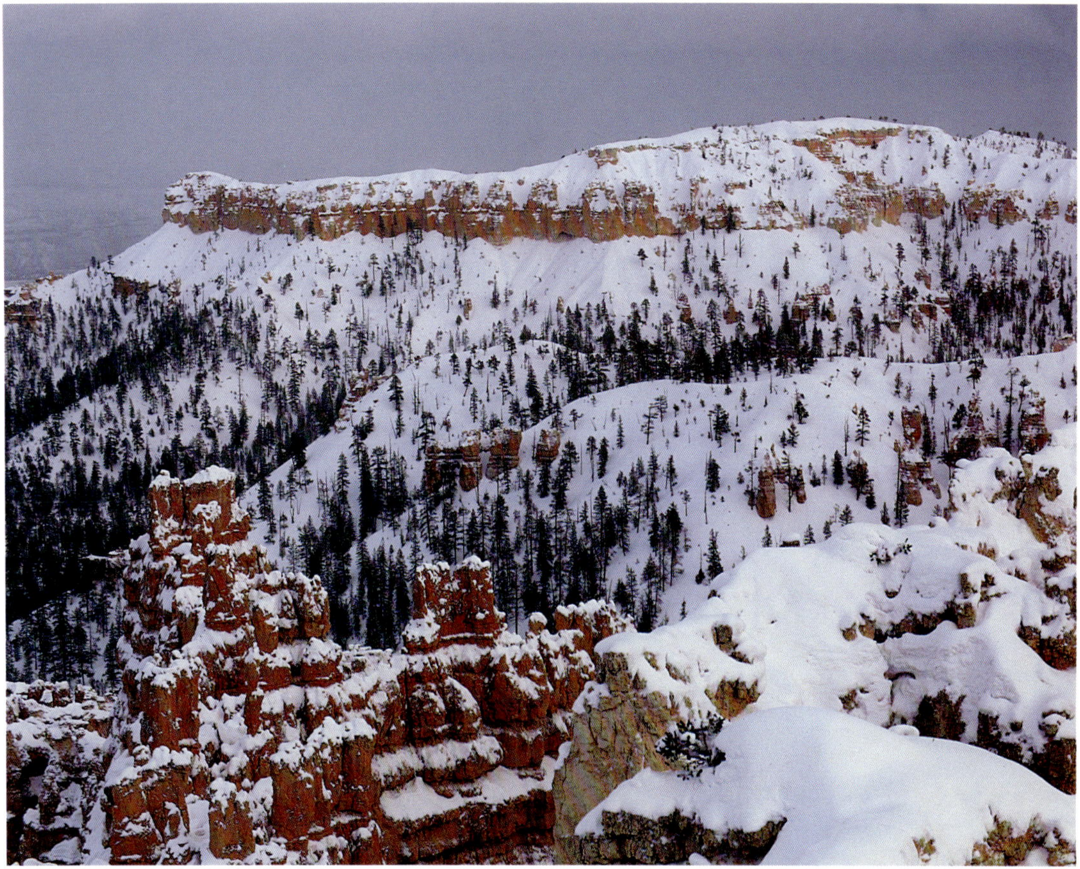

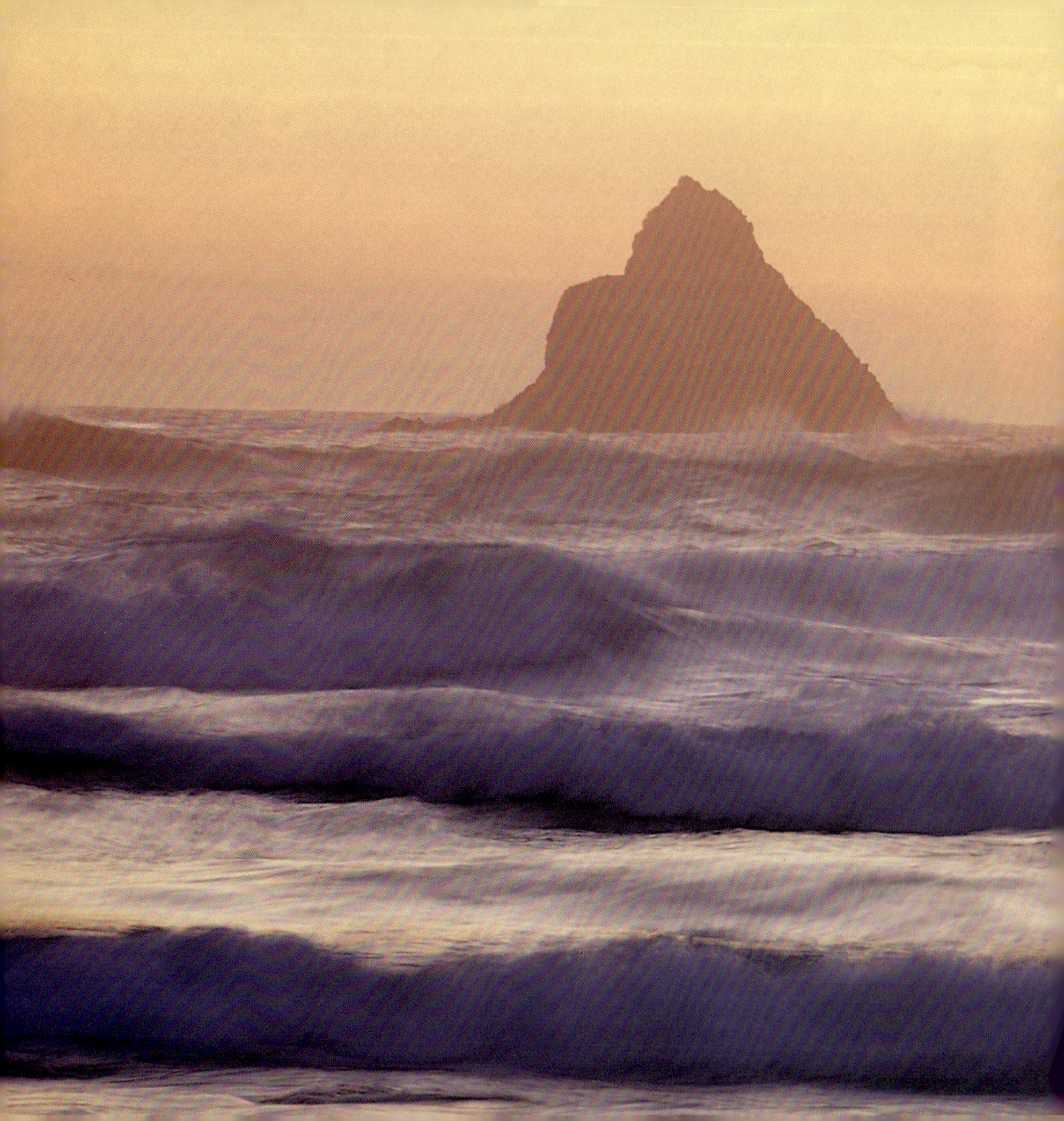

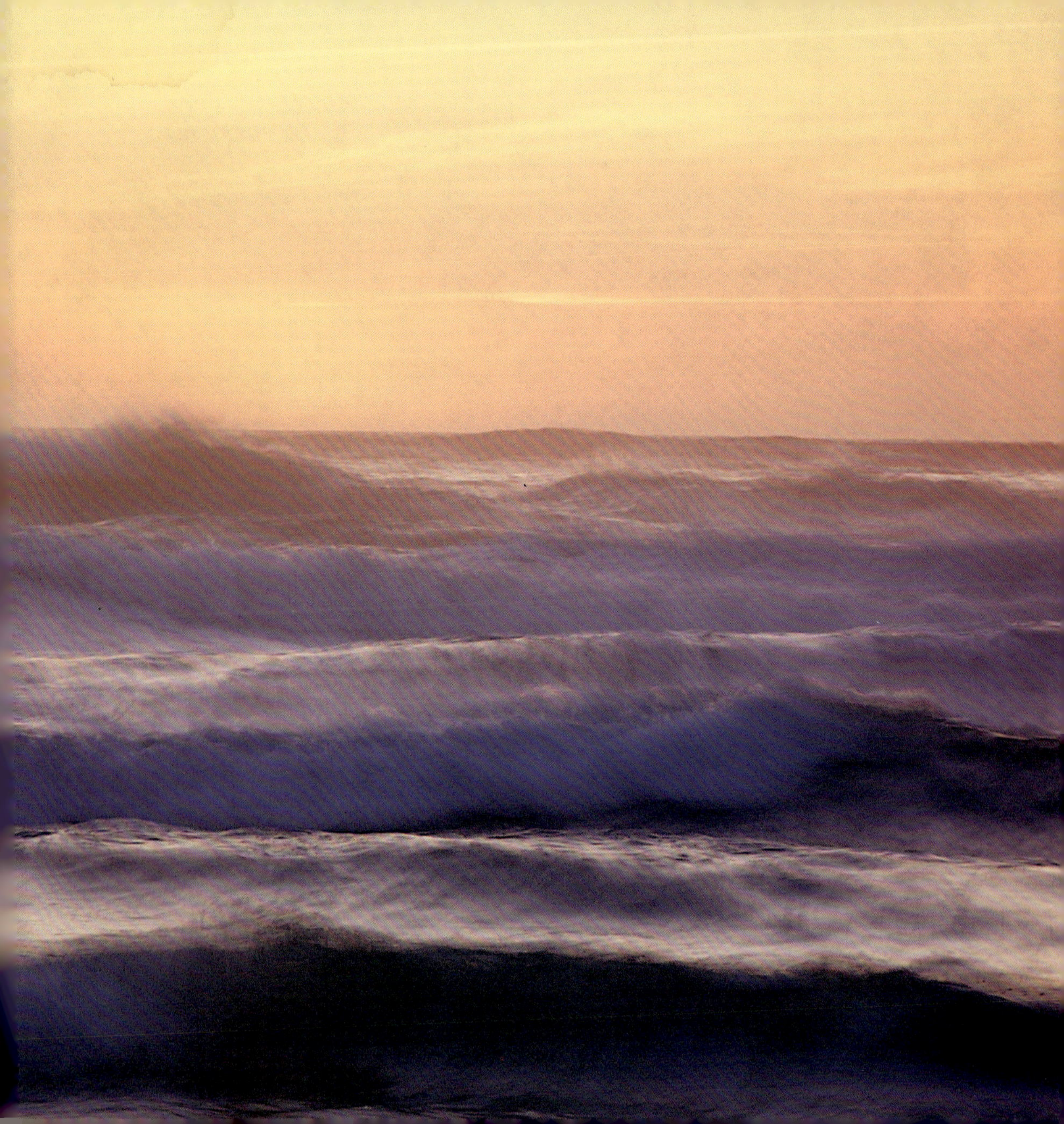

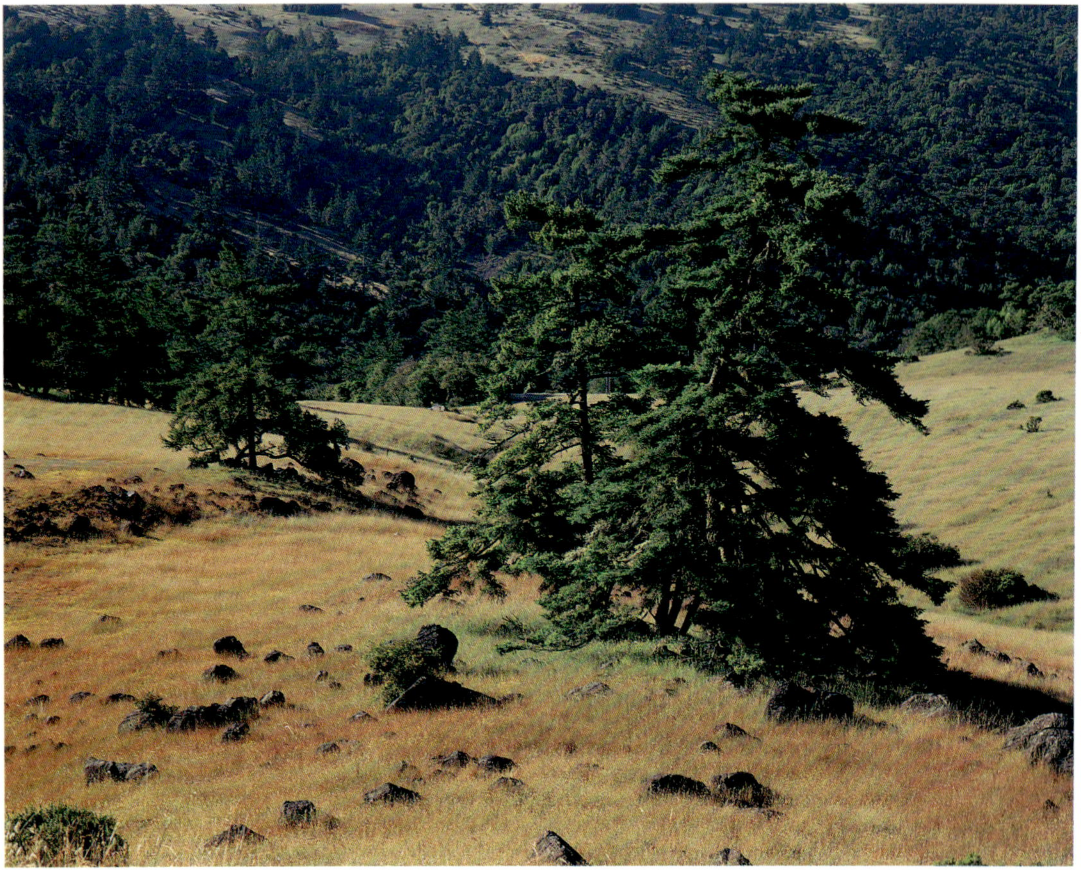

OceanSong
Occidental, California
A project of EcoCorps